ADHD:

The College Experience

how to make it through college
and reach your potential
by embracing your unique strengths

ARASH ZAGHI, PHD

as told to Connie Mosher Syharat

First Published: June 2018

Revised: January 2019

This book is dedicated to:

*my daughter Raha, the love of my life,
whose beauty in mind, body, and spirit inspires me to
work toward a better world for all children,*

*and to three extraordinarily strong, exceptionally
accomplished,
and tremendously supportive women in my life:*

*first, to Sarira, my cherished other half
whose love and wisdom have kept me on track,
and whose many strengths have provided balance
for my many shortcomings,*

ॐ

*to my mom, whose love and compassion
have helped me to believe in myself, and whose
steady guidance has molded me into a better person,*

ॐ

*and to my sister, whose reassurance, care,
and unconditional love have been a light in the darkness
during my most challenging times.*

ॐ

*Only in my wildest imagination could I have achieved my
goals without your support and encouragement. You
have inspired me with your strength and courage.
Because of you, I am proud to call myself a feminist.*

Here's to the crazy ones. The misfits. The rebels. The troublemakers. The round pegs in the square holes. The ones who see things differently. They're not fond of rules. And they have no respect for the status quo. You can quote them, disagree with them, glorify or vilify them. About the only thing you can't do is ignore them. Because they change things. They push the human race forward. And while some may see them as the crazy ones, we see genius. Because the people who are crazy enough to think they can change the world, are the ones who do.

- Steve Jobs

CONTENTS

AUTHOR'S NOTE

My own ADHD was not diagnosed until I had already finished my studies and was beginning a new career as a professor of engineering. I felt like a circus performer, juggling a whole bunch of flaming batons or huge knives, or maybe huge flaming knives. The stakes were really high, and I often felt totally overwhelmed and anxious. I knew I was trying to keep too many things up in the air and at some point in the future, I was going to drop something and get burned. But after my diagnosis, I began to understand why I have some of these challenges. Most importantly, I stopped blaming myself for making so many spelling errors in my emails, making little mistakes in front of my classes, forgetting about important things, and trying to do everything at once.

Once I started learning more about ADHD, I read and heard a great deal of stories that validated my own experience. I wanted to share my new understanding with everyone who was important to me so that they could finally understand what I was going through. If you feel like running off and asking your parents or teachers to read this, too, that's great! I've included some required reading for parents and educators in the last two chapters. Just make sure you hold onto this book long enough to finish it yourself!

I have spent a lot of my time in the past few years working closely with students just like you. And the more students and families I have met, the more I have realized that just by finding each other, we are helping ourselves. We might think that we are the only ones who have had these kinds of experiences in school, but it turns out much of what we go through is common to us all. Just realizing that we are not alone and that we are so very alike in so many ways, can make a huge difference.

As I tried to learn more about myself, I also started to understand that many people with ADHD traits can be immensely creative. As an engineer, I know that we desperately need this kind of creative, out-of-the-box thinking to solve some of the huge challenges that are headed our way. With this in mind, I began to research the connection between ADHD and creativity, along with the importance of cognitive diversity in finding innovative solutions to the complex problems that we will face as a nation. The National Science Foundation has supported my work, and I have spent the past few years recruiting students with ADHD into engineering research.

The promise of hope is ultimately what inspired me to write this book. I'd like to share my experience, as someone who knows intimately what it is like to live with ADHD, and as a college professor who works with students who also struggle with the same challenges.

Once word got out that I was working with college students with ADHD in an engineering research environment, the floodgates opened. I have received email after email from students and their families about their struggles in school, about their creative potential, and about the hope they felt when they read my story. If this is a new perspective for you, I understand that sometimes it is hard to see the bright side when you have been dealing with so many frustrations for such a long time. The promise of hope is ultimately what inspired me to write this book. I'd like to share my experience, as someone who knows intimately what it is like to live with ADHD, and as a college professor who works with students who also struggle with the same challenges.

I want to let you know that you can, absolutely, be successful in college, even though the deck is quite literally stacked against you. Surprisingly, a lot of the challenges that students with ADHD face have little to do with attention or hyperactivity. Our education system is designed for the majority of learners who can easily learn and think in more or less traditional ways. This means that there is a heavy emphasis on what you may not be good at, and very little that rewards what you *are* good at.

For learners with ADHD, even a simple thing like knowing how to study can be an issue that can derail us from success. Being forced to learn in the typical, linear fashion of a "normal" classroom can feel like torture: stay in your seat, stay on task, listen quietly, and follow the procedures. Since we think differently than most people, we present a challenge to the way things are. Many teachers may not understand that the system needs to change, or they don't want to change the way they do things. Even for those who are willing, the system leaves them feeling unable to make the changes that they know are necessary for their students. To top this off, many teachers don't have enough training or experience with diverse thinking styles to really understand us and what kind of environment we need to thrive.

Further complicating the situation, curriculum in public schools is often driven by standardized tests. Non-standard learners generally do not perform well on standardized tests, which creates yet another barrier for diverse thinkers. Diane Ravitch, a well-known researcher and critic of the education system, puts it nicely when she says, "Sometimes, the most brilliant and intelligent minds do not shine in standardized tests because they do not have standardized minds."

So, as we go through this standard education system, we must find our own non-standard ways to shine, and stop putting the blame entirely on ourselves for the difficulties that we have. We aren't standard thinkers, and we weren't built to sit still. We jump from one thing to another, faster than most people can follow. Our minds are constantly scanning the environment for novel and exciting experiences.

We think in unusual ways and we often do the unexpected. Because of this ability to surprise and innovate, we can be a pretty interesting group of inventors, artists, comedians, builders, and entrepreneurs. Sometimes we feel like we don't fit in. Sometimes we feel like we should give up on ourselves, on going to college, or on taking those tough courses that we know we really want to take. A lot of times, it is hard. The struggles that come along with being a different kind of learner can definitely cause some problems along the way. But your difference can also help you to do some pretty awesome things, surprising yourself and everyone else in the process.

I'm not going to promise you some kind of magic solution to the struggles that you are facing. Even after several years, I am still challenged by certain aspects of living with ADHD and working as an engineering professor in a university. In fact, one of the things I enjoy the least is writing, which makes certain parts of my job really difficult. That's why I had a lot of help writing this book! I have found ways to work with my strengths and weaknesses to accomplish my goals. I've found that there are some things that have helped me and my students, and they may be able to help you to improve your performance in school.

Getting through college probably won't be easy. You might have to work twice as hard as a lot of other people. In fact, if you aren't ready to work hard, this is not the book for you. My message is intended for passionate students who are eager to succeed but find that even though they are trying, things are not working out the way they had hoped. If you are still struggling despite all your effort, then this book was written just for you. I encourage you to work even harder, to stop blaming yourself, and to embrace your strengths. You might find yourself going places you never dreamed were possible.

INTRODUCTION

This book does not claim to be a comprehensive reference book about the causes or symptoms of ADHD, and it won't provide you with exhaustive information about medications or treatments. In short, this is not a book that claims to have a "cure" for what is often seen as an illness. It is not a collection of checklists or tips for success, although some strategies and perspectives will be explored. Instead, you will find a combination of my thoughts, observations, and personal experiences. This is a view of ADHD from the inside, told by a college professor who not only works with students who have ADHD, but also lives with it day in and day out. This book does not approach ADHD from a therapeutic or medical model; those books have already been written. Instead, our story is concerned with the many ways, small and large, that ADHD can affect your success in a college setting. Specifically, this book attempts to answer the following question: How can students with ADHD embrace their unique potential, find joy in learning, and overcome the barriers that they will face in a college setting?

What is life like when you are a college student with ADHD? Like everyone else, you'll be juggling the many demands of course requirements, homework, projects, deadlines, and exams, but ADHD can make these many demands even more challenging. **Chapter 1** dives into the daily experiences of navigating the pressures and the emotional ups and downs that we can face in college.

Procrastination, forgetfulness, and mind-wandering can leave us feeling overwhelmed and discouraged, while our impulsivity can lead to unintended consequences. But our ADHD-related traits are also strengths that we can leverage for our success.

What are the strengths that come along with ADHD traits, and what is their purpose in the greater scheme of things? **Chapter 2** explores the genetic inheritance of people with ADHD and examines how our abilities have been selected through evolution to play a unique role in human societies. You may have learned that ADHD was a disorder, and it can feel that way. However, ADHD traits can be powerful driving forces for creativity and success, even if they may sound like liabilities. Flipping the script about ADHD can give us a new perspective about our unique abilities and potential.

Chapter 3 looks more in detail at our genetic inheritance and shows how our ADHD-related traits can be leveraged for success. Procrastination and inattention can lead to highly creative solutions, while our ability to hyperfocus on things that we enjoy can make us wildly productive when we are engaged. Our high energy and risk-taking can give us the drive and the willingness to explore new possibilities, while our impulsivity and intense emotions can lead us in surprising directions and take us on unexpected and exciting journeys.

Even when we are aware of our strengths, we may still struggle with making the most of our strengths and staying engaged in college. If we struggle with maintaining our motivation, how can we cope with the challenges of finding our purpose within an education system that is not designed with our needs in mind? **Chapter 4** explores some of the challenges of the college experience; course requirements, antiquated teaching methods, and other barriers within the education system can leave us feeling unmotivated and unengaged. How can we light the spark of our own desire to learn and leverage our innate curiosity to build meaning? What are the ways that we can integrate our unique abilities and passions into our learning, and approach even our most boring courses with a playful creativity that makes learning more joyful and innovation more likely?

What is life like when you are a college student with ADHD? Like everyone else, you'll be juggling the many demands of course requirements, homework, projects, deadlines, and exams, but ADHD can make these many demands even more challenging.

Even if we find ways to stay motivated and find joy in the learning process, our ADHD traits can sometimes derail us, despite our best intentions. In **Chapter 5**, we examine how some of our traits can pose difficulties for us and think about how self-awareness can help us to tackle some of these realities head-on. We will talk about how small slip-ups can lead to huge unintended consequences, how our emotions can get the better of us, and how impatience and forgetfulness can get us off track. We'll think about some practical things that we can do to minimize our difficulties, like making a schedule that meets our needs, and ways to build a social network that can keep us afloat and offer support when we are feeling overwhelmed.

I've also included a message for the parents who are reading this book. In **Chapter 6**, I'll share some thoughts and observations from a professor's perspective. How can you provide the support that will help your college student succeed? We'll look at how some of the more extreme reactions to a child's diagnosis with ADHD can cause difficulties for the student in a college setting. From denial, to making excuses, to hovering over every move the student makes, parents can have a tough time finding balance. As parents, how can we give our college-aged students the tools they need to become independent adults, navigate the education system, advocate for themselves, and find ways to cope with the difficulties they will surely face?

Finally, in **Chapter 7** I've included a challenge to the university faculty and educators who hope to build a greater understanding of their diverse group of students. How can we, as educators, move beyond our defensive preservation of the status quo and challenge the common practices that discriminate against the diverse thinkers that populate our classes? We'll discuss how altering our perceptions and preconceptions can allow us to create a learning environment that can help our students reach their highest potential and look at how we can embrace instruction methods that encourage exploration, diversity of thought, creative problem-solving, and innovation.

It is my hope that this book will help you to think differently about ADHD, and that it may help you recognize your unique potential. In the case of parents and educators, I hope that this book will help you to better understand how you can challenge yourselves to nurture the potential and the creative abilities of college students with ADHD.

In summary, it is my goal that we will work toward answering some of these very important questions:

o   What does life feel like for college students with ADHD?

o   Why does ADHD exist? What is the unique role of people with ADHD in society?

o   How can we understand our weaknesses and embrace our strengths?

o   What are the challenges that we face in a college setting?

o   How can we leverage our talents, nurture our unique potential, and find success in higher education, despite all the challenges?

o   How can parents support students with ADHD as they go through college?

o   How can educators challenge the status quo to nurture the unique abilities of students with ADHD?

- 1 -

THE COLLEGE EXPERIENCE

Surviving college can be challenging for any student, but for those of us with ADHD, making it through even that first semester may seem next to impossible. The onslaught of boring courses that you *have* to take during freshman and sophomore year so that you can meet the graduation requirements, endless sets of apparently irrelevant homework assignments, and exams that seem to only test your ability to memorize and regurgitate the contents of an entire textbook can push you closer and closer to the edge. In this chapter, we will get into the reality of college life with ADHD. Whether you're putting things off until the last minute, forgetting important assignments, or making impulsive decisions, you may find yourself dealing with a lot of unintended consequences. All these ups and downs are like an emotional roller coaster that leaves you feeling out of control and all alone on a wild ride. While everyone's experience is different, don't be surprised if you see yourself in at least some of these stories. You're certainly not alone!

Burning the Midnight Oil

Imagine it's the night before your twenty-page final paper is due in your freshman writing seminar and you've been procrastinating for weeks. Now, you are ready to finally start researching the hideously boring topic that was assigned. You decide to begin by tidying up your desk area just a bit. Once you have cleared off and wiped down your desk, cleaned the lint out of the corners of your drawers, sorted out your pens and pencils, and put a load of dirty socks in the wash, you finally sit down to write the first paragraph. Because you want things to look *just right*, you decide to spend some time perfecting the font style and making sure that your title is exactly the right size. Exactly 78 minutes later, you've got the perfect look for your paper. But... still only one paragraph. Maybe you need to find just a few more sources to flesh out your argument, so you open the web browser one more time and start surfing the web.

Two hours later, you suddenly realize that you've spent the entire time learning about how nanorobotics might cure cancer, how artificial intelligence is probably going to destroy the world, and the mating habits of bonobo monkeys in the wild. All absolutely useful information, of course, but now you only have four hours left to pull together the rest of that paper. As time goes by, you begin to feel the lights of your clock blazing out at you like lasers. You desperately want to start writing the next paragraph, but you just can't seem to start the sentence.

Several nerve-wracking minutes pass while you struggle with what to write next. The longer you sit at the keyboard, the more impossible it seems that you will ever complete the assignment. It is 5 am, you are not even half-way done, and you realize that you have completely underestimated the amount of time it would take to write the paper. If battling chronic procrastination is something that sounds familiar (and I bet it does) rest assured that you are not the only one.

I've certainly been there, and so has just about everyone else whom I know who has ADHD. This is just the way that we are wired.

Chaos and Clutter

One of the shared experiences of many of us with ADHD is the presence of piles and piles of *stuff*. Somehow you may still have an awareness of where many of your things are in these piles. If you know that your toenail clippers are under your calculus textbook, which is hidden by your favorite black hoodie that is crumpled in the corner of your room, you know what I mean. There may be stacks of papers and notebooks on the floor, the bottom of your backpack may have a thick layer of crumpled worksheets and gum wrappers that have been crushed beneath your Biology textbook, and you may need to wade through a foot-deep flood of dirty laundry to make it across your dorm room. The remnants of a half-finished art project are spread out across your desk, surrounded by packages of metal trinkets, a spool of fishing line, needle-nosed plyers, and a hot glue gun.

To everyone else, it might look like a scene straight out of a post-apocalyptic novel: *Garbage was strewn across the bleak horizon. The survivors, clad in their full-body protective suits, searched the ruin, scavenging anything that might be of use: bits of wire, a blank notebook, a slightly scorched pair of Neoprene boots...* To you, this is just normal. Your roommates, however, have marked a line in duct tape across the floor in a semi-successful effort to contain the chaos of your overflowing laundry basket, but your still-damp towels are slowly creeping across the border as if they have a mind of their own.

Of course, everyone is different, and your reality may not be quite this disastrous. In fact, some of us may compensate by developing strong organizational skills, habits, or rituals to keep our things in order. Still, many of us do struggle with maintaining organization in our daily lives. From our paperwork to our clothes closet, we may feel the effects of our tendency to avoid tasks that do not appeal to us. If we aren't motivated to do our laundry, then we'll probably just order some brand-new socks and underwear online and then find something more enjoyable to do.

There may be stacks of papers and notebooks on the floor, the bottom of your backpack may have a thick layer of crumpled worksheets and gum wrappers that have been crushed beneath your Biology textbook, and you may need to wade through a foot-deep flood of dirty laundry to make it across your dorm room.

Even those who pride themselves on their organizational skills may find that it takes *a lot* of extra effort to attain the clear desk, the orderly binder of chemistry notes, or the organized dresser drawer. This lack of organization can lead us to lose track of important class materials and assignments, which in turn can affect our GPAs. Some of us have figured out ways to cope with this, with varying amounts of success. But if you haven't managed to get yourself organized quite yet, at the very least you know that you and your messy dorm room are in good company.

Distraction and Disappointment

Even if we have the best intentions, our brain's wiring can leave us feeling distracted, forgetful, and frustrated. Take the following scenario. Every class, you *start* out taking the neatest and most organized notes, but as the teaching assistant starts talking faster, your notes get messier. Gradually, your notes end up evolving into a highly detailed doodle of the Mars rover in all its glory creeping across the desolate landscape while mysterious three-eyed life forms with pointy teeth peek out at it from behind rocks. Or maybe you are not a doodler, but it's simply hard for you to both take notes *and* focus on what the teaching assistant in your physics class is saying. So, you get notes from a friend, and then you plan to meet with the TA to go over one of the problems. You talk with her after class and set a meeting for 2 pm on Friday. You know it is important, so you put it into the calendar on your phone and set an alert for two hours ahead of time to be sure you will be there, as scheduled.

Friday morning comes, and you see your reminder, right on time. A few minutes later you get a text from a friend. A group is heading over to the student union to grab lunch. It's been too long since you've spent some time with your friends, so you decide to go with them and end up hanging out all afternoon. Without you noticing, the time for your meeting has come and gone. A couple of days later, you get out your notes to study. A sick feeling washes over you as you remember the meeting that never actually happened. You are afraid to send an email to the TA to apologize, since you are sure that she will think you are a slacker and that you just blew her off on purpose. People who don't know you might assume that if you have forgotten something, that it's not important to you. But when you have ADHD, forgetting something doesn't mean you don't care about it. Sometimes, despite your best intentions, you will get distracted by other things and forget to do something that you really do care about.

The Labyrinth

We all have the potential to get sidetracked by our wandering minds, no matter where we are or what we are supposed to be doing. You could be on a simple mission to grab something from the fridge when it strikes. You open the door to the fridge, when you suddenly begin to contemplate ordering a new chain for your bicycle so that it will stop making that horrible grinding sound when you shift from first to second gear. You imagine how you can remove the old chain and start thinking about the design. It is so fascinating how you can open one of the links to put it on your bike, but oddly enough, these links never break when you are pedaling.

This train of thought gets you pondering the ways that you could use the links of the old bike chain for some creative artwork for the guest room. This would definitely impress your dad's friend. He is an amazing architect who will be coming for a visit soon. The thought of his impending visit brings you back to your last family camping trip, when he came along and brought his daughter. You break out into a sweat as you remember how embarrassed you were when you almost set his daughter's dress on fire because you had thought it would be fun to pour some kerosene into the camp fire. You blink and find yourself still standing there 10 minutes later, shivering in the cold air and holding a package of cream cheese in front of the open fridge. You feel completely confused about what you were doing there in the first place. You put the cream cheese back in the drawer and walk away. You had meant to grab something for lunch, but due to your sudden trip down memory lane, you never actually did it. Then, two hours later your stomach starts growling and you wonder why you feel so hungry.

After 15 years of marriage, my wife knows better than to believe me if I tell her that I am heading to the hardware store for half an hour to buy some screws, a drill bit, and some WD-40. She knows full well that I will be gone for at least three hours because I will be completely lost in a haze of creative inspiration, wandering from aisle to aisle. I will eventually return with no screws or drill bit, but instead with a dimmable LED lamp, a spool of shiny brass wire, and $300 worth of materials for a home-improvement project that I immediately start but may never finish. If she actually does need me to come back at a certain time with specific items, she will send my 8-year-old daughter along with me carrying written instructions to remind me of the shopping list and the time that I need to get home. We all have had these kinds of experiences, and these moments can sometimes make us doubt our sanity. Still, I know that getting lost in the labyrinth of my thoughts allows me space to explore the many possibilities in my mind to create in new and unexpected ways.

My Way or the Highway

Our wiring gives us a strong need to do what rewards us on a personal level. This means that we have a very hard time getting started on tasks that aren't interesting to us, but we can go all out if it is something that sparks our curiosity. This also means that sometimes we can disregard parts of a project that just don't get us going and instead focus on the parts that get us really excited. Doing things in our own way *can* help us to create something unique, but it can also negatively affect our grades if our instructors do not allow us the freedom to deviate from the given instructions.

The fact that our brains are wired to respond when we are deeply interested in something means that we sometimes face difficulties because we have a tendency to do things "our way," no matter what.

For example, it's Tuesday afternoon, and you're sitting down in your dorm room to review the instructions for your Architectural Design final project. You've been assigned to work on designing a new downtown center for a small city that has been struggling to revitalize its local economy. The project instructions call for a focus on creating a community space that is designed to draw small businesses to the area while creating a vibrant and active space for locals and tourists alike. The thought of creating an exciting community space like this really gets your brain going. In fact, you kick it into overdrive and get started right away.

You spend hours and hours brainstorming ideas and penciling designs in your sketch pad. Since you love design, you are passionate about the environment, and you are also an avid skater, you find yourself coming up with all sorts of fantastic ideas for gardens, solar panels and green roof spaces, and skate parks. After spending a great deal of time working on these designs, you notice that you've strayed quite a bit from the focus on designing a vibrant city space full of businesses, restaurants, and trendy shops.

Still, you know that since you are following your passions, your project will showcase your best work. You're so psyched about your ideas that they just keep on flowing out in an unstoppable tide. Your final design presents a comprehensive plan that turns a decaying city center into a refreshing green space where the local residents will enjoy spending time with friends and family. The design is beautiful and very well thought out, and you hand it in, feeling absolutely sure that you are going to score an A on the project.

Two weeks later, you receive your grade. You are devastated to find out that even though your professor loved your work, your project received a lower grade than you expected because you didn't follow the instructions. You feel that you did your best, but your grade doesn't reflect the amount of time and effort that you put into the project. You got so excited about your own ideas that you ignored a key part of the project! The fact that our brains are wired to respond when we are deeply interested in something means that we sometimes face difficulties because we have a tendency to do things "our way," no matter what.

We might end up at the center of conflict in a group project because we have trouble compromising on a certain detail or we might get marked down on our homework because we insist on solving math or physics problems in our own way. Or, we may be given a solution to a problem, but still insist on doing the whole thing from scratch so that we will learn from the experience of doing it ourselves. While our strong need to work in the way that feels best to us can help us to put our all into our work, it can still sometimes negatively impact our academics because we may not always be willing to follow the guidelines that have been set for us.

In disciplines like STEM fields that reward linear thinking and following procedures in a certain way, doing things our own way isn't always helpful to our grades. In fact, our creative process is often undervalued, or even discouraged. Still, it is important for us to know that there is strength in our ability to disregard and challenge the status quo. Even though our way might not always be the most efficient, and it certainly won't always earn us the grade we are hoping for, it is still important for us to follow our own path and find new ways to tackle complex problems. By following those almost unstoppable urges to do things our own way, we can go beyond the confines of what we are told to do, make the most of our ability to focus on what gets us excited, and create in new and unexpected ways.

The Rollercoaster

I'm sure you have had times when you feel that your mind is making you feel out of control and completely overwhelmed about everything that you have to do. You know that you need to study for your calculus exam, but you have three sets of physics homework to hand in this week, plus you have a lab report to write, and 100 pages to read for English. On top of this, you need to meet with your advisor and submit your plan of study, plus actually *go* to class, and still find time to eat and sleep. All your responsibilities are swirling around in your mind like a carnival ride gone wrong. You can't seem to make it stop long enough for you to figure out which one is the most important. Prioritizing all these tasks just seems impossible.

Understanding how your brain works may help you to stop blaming yourself for reacting to things the way you do. This way, you don't have to let feelings of anger, guilt, and embarrassment drive your actions and reactions.

After some deliberation, you decide to go with the reading, but then find yourself zoning out repeatedly, having to reread entire passages over and over and still struggling to remember anything. In your head, your calculus book is still circling, looking like that scary clown from IT. Your lab report is in there too, and all of that other stuff that you have to do has all sprouted fangs and is gnashing its pointy teeth at you from the corners of your imagination. How will you possibly get all of this done? In the end, you've spent so much time worrying about what to do that you haven't been able to finish half of it, and your grades suffer. ADHD makes it hard for us to prioritize and get started on our tasks, and this makes college a serious challenge. Most of us with ADHD will feel completely overwhelmed at one time or another. Remember this: it's not just you, and it's not your fault. These kinds of discouraging experiences can feel like repeated resounding smacks to the face of your self-esteem. There's a good chance that you will start mentally kicking yourself about how badly you have messed up everything. You will feel completely discouraged, as if no matter how hard you try, things just don't work out for you. You may feel like dropping out of your course or giving up on college entirely. Believe it or not, this tendency to feel like the world is ending because of a minor failure is not unique to you either. Most of us have faced this deep level of discouragement at one time or another.

ADHD can make our emotions super intense, and it can also make us pay extra attention to these super strong feelings. Forget making mountains out of mole hills. Some of us make our mole hills into massive lava and ash-spewing volcanoes. These emotional eruptions can produce dark clouds that hang over our moods and cast a shadow over our decisions. Let me be clear, even if you understand how ADHD can affect your emotions, it is pretty close to impossible to manage these emotions when something blindsides you. All the energy in your brain will still go right to that emotional circuit, and you'll still feel every single bit of those feelings. But at the very least, understanding how your brain works may help you to stop blaming yourself for reacting to things the way you do. This way, you don't have to let feelings of anger, guilt, and embarrassment drive your actions and reactions.

The Odd One Out

Going off to college usually means leaving everything and everyone you know behind and starting out fresh. Since many of us have difficulties making and maintaining friendships, the transition to college can leave us feeling alone and unsure of how to connect with others. Even when we do make new friends, we may seem aloof or inattentive to them since we often struggle with keeping in touch or remembering important things, like our friend's birthday, for example.

Imagine that you've become friends with a girl who lives next door to you in the dorm. You see her *all the time* and have started hanging out together on weekends and even studying together for the physics course that you both are taking. After the semester ends, however, you no longer have any classes together. Plus, you find out that she has decided to move out of the dorm into an apartment of her own due to a disagreement with her roommate.

You both agree to keep in touch, and since she's only moved about ten minutes away, this doesn't seem like too much of a challenge. Still, now that your friend is out of sight, she is also, unfortunately, out of mind. It seems like the most difficult thing in the world to call her on the phone. Like many of us, you find phone calls anxiety-provoking and unenjoyable, so you avoid them. You'd much rather just text her to hang out, and you mean to do it, but it slips your mind. Days turn to weeks, and now you feel so guilty that you haven't been in touch that you avoid it even more. By the time you run into her at the local café, you've grown apart enough that you say hi, but don't even stop to talk to each other. You hear from another friend that she is upset with you for not hanging out anymore, so you give up on the friendship and move on.

These kinds of social misunderstandings can make it harder for us to build the connections that help us to be successful in our classes. Many people make and keep friends easily so they have no trouble finding someone to team up with on a class project or to study with for the final exam. But since we often struggle with our social lives, we may end up studying on our own or not knowing anyone who we can ask for help with the class notes. Even though you might feel like the odd one out sometimes, you should know that many of us go through the same thing.

Pulling the Alarm

On top of dealing with the stress of college courses and the emotional ups and downs of your daily life, you might also end up in some difficult situations because you sometimes act on impulse in ways that defy all logic. Impulsive behavior can range anywhere from spending all of your pay check on a Yoda Halloween costume for your puppy to pulling the fire alarm in your dorm after having a few drinks on Thursday night. You might not even know why you are doing these things. You are walking back from the bathroom, when your eye is suddenly caught by a little red handle on the wall. In the blink of an eye, you reach out and pull it. Next thing you know, there you are in your fleece ducky pajamas, standing outside in a snowstorm with your friends. Your brain didn't even give you the chance to stop and think about the potential consequences of your actions. You saw it. You did it. And now you are in for a world of trouble.

There is a culture of "boys will be boys" that shrugs off the impulsive actions of the guys as no big deal, but the consequences of impulsive behavior can be much more far-reaching for young women, since they have to face both the results of their actions and the fact that they aren't living up to the cultural expectations for "how a girl should act." Sometimes your impulses don't seem like such a big a deal, but even little things can add up to more trouble than you anticipated.

Maybe your professor asks you to bring in your laptop, so you can try out the new math software during class, but instead of following along, you find yourself online, ordering a new set of extra-long false eyelashes and a *really* nice pair of wireless headphones to replace the ones you lost the week before. Then you start thinking about your best friend from fifth grade. You start wondering what she is up to and find yourself posting a questionable photo of yourself to her page on social media. Now you have not only missed half of the class and the instructions about the software you were supposed to be learning about, but you've also racked up a bit more credit card debt and embarrassed yourself on social media in the process.

If you have ever done something on impulse and then been unable to explain the reason why to your teachers, your parents (or yourself), then count yourself as a card-carrying member of the ADHD VIP club. At some point, we all have to deal with the unintended and unanticipated consequences of our impulses. However, you should also know that given the right situation, your ability to make quick decisions can sometimes work to your advantage.

Silver Linings

We all experience these things to varying degrees. Many people, even those without ADHD, may relate to these experiences to some extent. But for us, these stories are woven right into the fabric of our daily lives. They are, and have always been, with us because they are wired into our very being. So, if you have felt like you've seen a little bit of yourself in these examples, you are in good company. I know that going through difficult situations in college can leave us feeling discouraged and willing to give up. Many of the self-help books out there present such a dismal picture that it can be hard to see how there can possibly be any benefits to living with ADHD.

But despite the difficulties, there is a bright side. The same traits that can cause so much struggle for us can also contribute to some absolutely brilliant moments. There will be a time when you pull off the most amazing project because a crazy idea comes to you at three in the morning. Your brain will get so excited that you work for hours without eating or drinking or even checking Instagram. You'll bring something unique to class that catches the attention of your professor, you'll end up solving a problem in a completely unexpected way, or you'll make an animation that gets you an A because it was *so insanely* creative. We will discuss this more in Chapter 3, which will explore how we can use our innate strengths to our benefit in school, in our careers, and in our lives.

To break the mold and challenge the status quo, you've got to be willing to risk your own reputation, the rejection of others, and sometimes, even your own physical safety. We do these things naturally, and our unparalleled ability to take calculated risks gives us the potential to be innovators in whatever we do.

You are a college student with ADHD. And there are certain difficulties that come with the territory. But you have an ability to think outside of the box and a willingness to do the unexpected. Your ADHD gives you strengths that you can use to your advantage, despite what everyone else may be telling you. There are more and more stories in the news about people with ADHD who channeled their high energy into fame, fortune, and success. Michael Phelps directed his energy into swimming and became the most decorated Olympian of all time. Actress Michelle Rodriguez has capitalized on her strengths and has been battling zombies in the movies ever since. Comedian and actor Jim Carrey credits ADHD for giving him a sense of humor like no other. Even Beyoncé's little sister, Solange, a successful singer and now a Grammy winner, says that she has a naturally high energy level due to her ADHD. Some might say that these people were successful in spite of their ADHD traits, but all of them credit ADHD with being at least part of what makes them so unique.

In addition to their uniqueness, creativity, and high energy, all of these people had the willingness to take a risk to do something extraordinary. And while we can't say definitively that famous figures from the past had ADHD traits, history is full of great examples of scientists and thinkers who couldn't have achieved what they did without the willingness to take tremendous risks. Ben Franklin standing outside in a thunderstorm with his kite is one example. The Wright brothers risking their lives to build and test a functional airplane is another. To break the mold and challenge the status quo, you've got to be willing to risk your own reputation, the rejection of others, and sometimes, even your own physical safety. We do these things naturally, and our unparalleled ability to take calculated risks gives us the potential to be innovators in whatever we do.

Of course, you might not end up being rich and famous, but at least you know that it is possible to set your goals high. For now, you've just got to worry about getting through college, and that means understanding how and why your brain works the way it does so that you can embrace your strengths.

- 2 -

FLIPPING THE SCRIPT

You've probably heard a lot about ADHD, but have you actually ever stopped and asked yourself what this whole ADHD thing is about? What is the purpose? Why would nature design a set of traits that makes life so frustrating for those of us who are wired differently than most people? Most books will not answer this question and will instead focus on explaining all the different "symptoms" and their possible causes. You will probably read about differences in brain structure, neurotransmitters, and environmental factors that contribute to ADHD. These can all be important, and they *are* part of the conversation, but many books will leave out ADHD's role in human evolution. These books are often written by psychologists from the perspective that ADHD is a defect. They will make you believe that something is wrong with you and then they'll try to help you figure out how to "fix" yourself. This negative narrative can make you think that ADHD is just an unlucky random genetic mutation. Read any book about it and count the "d-words" that you find: disability, dysfunction, disorder, deficit, and disease. This narrative, as it is told by doctors, psychologists, and special educators is incomplete.

Despite their intentions to help people, many professionals are still overlooking a key piece of the ADHD puzzle. In this chapter I would like to share a different perspective that can help you understand why ADHD is an advantage and why it is generally perceived otherwise. Get ready to rethink everything that you think you know about ADHD. I want you to consider the possibility that you can learn to develop your strengths and use them to your benefit instead of fighting against yourself all the time. I hope you will find this information refreshing, and possibly, so exciting that you will want to run around like crazy and show it to all your friends and family. I know you might be thinking, "Great. Another positive thinking book." Trust me, I know there are more than enough of those around! I am not trying to paint a rosy picture of things or imply that if you think hard enough you can change yourself into someone else. What I *am* trying to do is help you to reframe the way you look at ADHD by sharing some of the information that changed my life for the better, made me realize my own strengths, and most importantly, helped me to stop blaming myself. I believe that by understanding why your brain works in certain ways, you can find ways to benefit from your unique abilities to succeed in college and beyond.

Survival of the Fittest

One of the first steps in understanding your brain is getting to the bottom of the question of ADHD genes and why they are so persistent in populations all over the world. Research on ADHD genes shows that they have undergone positive selection. This means that nature has chosen the genes related to ADHD for some reason. If these traits are, as we are consistently told, so horribly disadvantageous, then wouldn't they just gradually be eliminated through natural selection and disappear from humanity? Survival of the fittest is merciless. If an adorable little monkey can't climb fast enough or hide well enough, it is going to be lunch for someone. And if it has been turned into monkey nuggets by a hungry predator, then it definitely won't be passing on its genes to the next generation, no matter how cute it is.

So, why is ADHD still hanging around in the human gene pool and messing with your ability to focus on your professor's lecture? The answer to this seeming contradiction may be this: ADHD is still here because it is a set of traits that have been passed down from our hunter-gatherer ancestors because they are *beneficial* to society. Our brains are like this because we inherited genes that exist to support the survival of the human race. When people find themselves in crisis situations that seem impossible, typical brains may not be able to find a way out or wouldn't dare to take the huge risks necessary to escape. And that's where we come in.

Risk and Reward

You might be wondering how and why ADHD is passed down from our ancestors. Certain genes are related to ADHD traits, and they are *highly* hereditary. If you were looking for some way to blame your parents for all of the inexplicable things you did in your life, here is your big chance. Just kidding. We're not blaming anyone, right? Still, the genetics for ADHD do tend to run in families. If your mom, or your dad, or your identical twin has ADHD, then there's a higher than average likelihood that you do, too. One key example of this genetic link is the 7R allele (the seven-repeat variation) of the DRD4 gene, which is strongly associated with ADHD. The 7R variation of this gene contains the blueprint for dopamine receptors that are less sensitive than most to dopamine.

Dopamine is a neurotransmitter that is involved in focus, reward, and motivation. Dopamine helps by offering your brain a reward to make you feel good. If your brain is less responsive to dopamine, then you will need higher levels of it to feel motivated and engaged. In fact, you'll need higher levels of dopamine for your brain to feel rewarded for whatever it is doing. Think about it. What do you enjoy? Skydiving? Video gaming? Really spicy food? Running marathons? There is something really intense that gets your brain excited. Just like our hunter-gatherer ancestors, we thrive on high-risk, high-stimulation situations. DRD4-7R seems to be at least partially responsible for the traits that drive people to seek new experiences, to be highly active, to be insatiably curious, and to take risks.

The traits of distractibility, impulsivity, and risk-taking were likely some of the traits needed to survive and keep a full belly in a hunter-gatherer society. When a group is faced with a sudden environmental change or a sudden decrease in an expected food source, the risk-takers are the ones who lead the charge in finding ways to cope with these challenges. If your people were facing a famine, would you be willing to take a drastic risk (like crossing an ocean in a tiny wooden ship) to possibly survive? It has been noted that populations that have migrated long distances have a higher rate of ADHD genetics. The important thing to understand is that while these traits can lead to some seriously risky situations for individual people, they can also be a benefit to you and to society, depending on the situation.

Let's take food as an example. On campus, you might think that the dining hall food is gross, but you're probably not starving. At the very least, you know you can get by with a 25-cent pack of ramen noodles and a microwave. But let's take it back several millennia and imagine that you are part of a hunter-gatherer society on the brink of running out of food, and there's not a pack of spicy noodles to be found anywhere. Let's imagine that most of the members of your group are pretty predictable people. They don't do many unexpected things and they have a reputation for being stable and reliable.

When food gets scarce, most people might stick to what they know or try hunting for small animals that won't gore them to death with massive tusks. They would probably wander the forest looking for more of the same kinds of nuts and berries, and generally they would try to play it safe. They wouldn't think to sample the shiny red berries that grow on the side of the cliff because a) they never strayed off the main path or got close enough to the edge of the cliff to even *notice* that there might be berries growing there, b) their mama always told them that eating mysterious red berries could get them killed, and c) even if they *did* get close enough to the cliff to notice the berries, falling into a ravine just to get a snack would probably seem like a horrible trade-off.

Most of your tribe is made up of these more risk-averse people, but there are a few of you who are always pushing the limits of everything by doing things that probably seem crazy to everyone else. You and your buddies have already explored the entire forest, navigated the dark depths of the caves, and climbed to the tops of the tallest trees. You know that there are absolutely, without a doubt, no more walnuts, lingonberries, boysenberries, or gooseberries anywhere. For some reason, you didn't listen to your mom when she told you not to go near the edge of the cliff. You have already been up and down the cliff several times without a rope and noticed the bushes that were growing there. Now that your family is faced with a food shortage, you make the snap decision to go back down the cliff and you happen to find tons of ripe, red berries just waiting to be eaten. Without thinking about it too much, you impulsively pop a few of them in your mouth to see how they taste.

Obviously, there are lots of bad ways this situation can end. Your foot might slip on a loose stone while climbing down the rocks, and you could plunge the 100 feet down to a gruesome death at the bottom of the ravine. Or, you might make it down the cliff due to your amazing free climbing skills, but then suffer a horrible untimely demise due to your enjoyment of the (*oops!*) highly toxic berries. The preferable ending to this situation is that because you didn't follow the rules, you've discovered the one delicious fruit snack that your family can survive on temporarily, until someone (probably also you) manages to hunt and kill a wild boar.

In our example, we'll imagine that you are lucky, and you've discovered the one thing that can save your people from starvation. Now you just need to find a way to get this berry crop harvested and brought back to the village. You'll have to come up with a more efficient way to gather the berries. If you are the only one to go up and down the cliff to pick the berries, it will take forever to harvest them all and everyone will probably just go ahead and die of boredom while waiting for you to finish. In the end, you devise a thick, woven rope and some small baskets from the strong fibers of a grass that grows nearby. Then you carve a sort of pulley system from the wood of the nearest tree. Your system allows many others to aid in the harvest of the berries, and benefits everyone by enabling even those who are less willing to take risks to safely go up and down the most dangerous of cliffs.

The upshot of this scenario is that without the risk-takers, the folks who like to play it safe would most likely have died of starvation. The group needs a few risk-takers like us because everyone benefits from what we can find out through exploration. It's true, even when we discover things that harm us (like the fact that a berry contains a potent neurotoxin), others can still learn and benefit from what we have found. We can play a unique role in unearthing potentially valuable information that would otherwise remain unknown. I hope that this makes sense to you. Some things that we do might seem crazy and dangerous under normal circumstances, but they can actually be the very things that people need to do to survive an extreme event or situation.

A small number of explorers and risk-takers seems to be just about right in enabling groups of people to survive a crisis without losing too many members of the group. Not coincidentally, the percentage of people with ADHD is around 5%-10% across populations. It wouldn't make sense, from an evolutionary perspective, to have a society where everyone exhibited these traits. Imagine it! You'd try to go downtown to do some shopping, but the bus would never show up because the bus driver would have decided to go explore all the different routes to the beach, and the store shelves would be empty because the employees would have eaten all the chocolate bars and then forgotten to order more.

If no one is willing to go down the cliff, no one gets the tasty treats. But if everyone is willing to try the berries right off the bat, everyone risks death by poisoning. Because of the exploration by the cliff-climbers, the rest of the group learns not only that there is another potential source of food, but more importantly, whether the food source is, in fact, edible. Societies learn from both the mistakes and the discoveries of risk-takers.

Social Expectations

Now that we know that ADHD traits are essential for humanity to make it through challenging circumstances, we must ask ourselves another question. If these traits are so necessary for the survival of human societies, then why on earth are they seen so negatively now? It makes sense to look at how much societies have changed since the days when hunting and gathering were the dominant ways to find food. Once humans settled down and started farming, food sources were much more reliable. People felt much more secure, and suddenly the traits that were once seen as valuable for survival started to be seen as unnecessary, and even undesirable. When life in society settles down to a predictable "normal," people who are impulsive and unpredictable are called dangerous and crazy. This shift in social expectations and values, along with the genetic persistence of ADHD traits, can help us to understand why we can feel so at odds with our environment.

There is a huge mismatch between our traits and the expectations placed on us in today's society and particularly in school settings. It is true that our impulsiveness and risk-taking can be a liability to us as individuals, but they are also potentially assets to us and our peers, given the right circumstances. Our schools can squash our natural abilities to explore and discover. They are missing the opportunity to nurture and develop these extraordinary abilities by failing to encourage creativity and not allowing kids to do things differently. Our schools are too customized for "typical" and "standard" learners but are not equipped to nurture the abilities of those who think differently.

Lots of people are really good at solving problems after seeing sample step-by-step solutions. These learners might excel when following the rules, but they may then find themselves so constrained by these learned steps that they are unable to think outside of the box or consider alternative solutions to problems. As a university professor, I am all too familiar with learners who are either not able or do not dare to move beyond the boundaries of conventional thinking when faced with a difficult challenge, even though they have mastered the skills needed to ace all of their exams.

The way our society works might make us think that it has all been figured out, and that we humans have moved beyond the times where the traits of impulsivity and risk-taking might be a benefit for survival. Agricultural and industrial societies like ours thrive on orderly systems, patience, and sustained focus on tiny repetitive details. For these systems to function, workers must be able to perform repeated tasks, like attaching a wire to a certain machine part on a factory floor for 12 hours straight or plucking potatoes out of the dirt for an entire day. It's true that our society needs people who can do these types of work consistently and diligently, but we've also got to encourage those among us whose very nature demands a different course of action. If our system crushes the unique abilities that allow risk-taking and innovation in difficult times, we are also crushing our chances of surviving the next crises that are headed our way.

Now's the Time

Our society's dependence on fossil fuels is actively contributing to the creation of large-scale problems like climate change. We can expect new waves of disease outbreaks as the planet warms, natural habitats change, populations shift, and pathogens outsmart the antibiotics that we have been relying on for so long. Our growing dependence on interconnected computer networks adds to our already huge need for better cybersecurity. These massive challenges are extreme disasters just waiting to happen. When these crises occur, will linear thinking and incremental progress be enough? Will we be capable of the creative thinking that help us make the leap and find innovative solutions?

Now, more than possibly any other time in human history, we need people who are willing to defy norms and expectations in ways that can help us adapt and survive. Our society is changing rapidly, our scientific knowledge is expanding at an astoundingly swift pace, and our technological capacity is increasing exponentially. With these changes come new challenges that may be especially suited to our unique abilities. Since ADHD traits can allow us to constantly scan the environment for new information, while also giving us the willingness and impulsiveness to go out on a limb, we are the risk-takers, the explorers, the discoverers, and the entrepreneurs that can spur the changes we need to survive. As a society, we need to encourage and channel the traits that will help us face down the coming challenges, just as the ancient hunter faced down his prey. When you look at yourself in this way, you will see that the traits that *just don't work* in most classrooms can be a fountain of unlimited creative potential and energy that drives innovative thinking.

Now, more than possibly any other time in human history, we need people who are willing to defy norms and expectations in ways that can help us adapt and survive. Since ADHD traits allow us to constantly scan the environment for new information, while also giving us the willingness and impulsiveness to go out on a limb, we are the risk-takers, the explorers, the discoverers, and the entrepreneurs that can spur the changes we need to survive.

I hope that reading this chapter has allowed you to rethink what you have been told about why we are the way we are, and help you understand why our unique strengths are now being called a deficiency and a disorder. Over the course of 7 million years in the history of *Homo sapiens*, we have played a significant role in the survival of our race by finding new ways to survive sudden environmental changes and challenging circumstances. It is only in the past 10,000 years that society has changed so dramatically that our traits have come to be seen as a liability. We are now the square pegs that just won't fit into society's round holes.

Understanding this might not help you to get more organized, to suddenly start remembering to hand in your important assignments, or to rein in your impulsive decisions. The knowledge that you've got a special role to play in human evolution might not make you feel better when you've just locked yourself out of your dorm room for the fourth time this week. You're probably still going to feel like banging your head against a wall the next time you open up your backpack and realize that once again you've remembered to pack your laptop charger but left your laptop behind in your dorm room.

So, how does hearing this part of the story change anything? I want you to remember this story during the worst moments of your darkest days. There will be times when we feel so overwhelmed that we just want to give up. There will be times when the difficulties of managing life in college make you want to just hide in your room and put a pillow over your head. It is during these times that knowing your unique potential can be the tiny ray of light that pulls you back from the edge. Even if it just gives us the ability to accept ourselves for who we are, knowing our potential can help to keep us sane. We may have trouble dealing with the challenges of everyday life, but rest assured that programmed right into the fiber of our being is an extraordinary ability. Ultimately, society needs people like us to find a way through the larger-than-life challenges that every once in a while, may come our way.

- 3 -

YOUR CREATIVE POTENTIAL

In the past few years, I have led multiple research projects, funded by the National Science Foundation, to evaluate if creativity and ADHD are correlated. My research, along with several other studies, supports what you may already have begun to suspect: many people with ADHD are highly creative, scoring higher than their peers on measures that evaluate creativity. The unique way that our brains are wired gives us a high potential for out-of-the-box thinking. This kind of divergent thinking is critical for creative problem solving. Finding new ways of doing things involves drawing on the available resources and putting things together in new ways to create something unexpected. And since we often have a lot of things going on in our heads, we've got a lot of resources from which to draw.

One example of this can be found in the way we pay attention to our environment. If you have ADHD traits, your mind usually doesn't focus on just one thing. Our minds wander, registering anything and everything that is going on around us. Imagine that your mind is a fishing net being pulled through the water. Even if you aim to catch only a tuna, you may end up with an octopus, a few squid, and a dolphin, along with all sorts of other sea creatures, plus a bunch of garbage in your net. While others may then go through their nets and throw back the fish and empty bottles that they didn't mean to catch, we may just decide to keep it all and see what kind of soup we can make with it. We cast our attentional nets much wider than others, or alternatively, others may be more likely to sort through it all and chuck the garbage. Thus, we may end up with much more input from our environment that we do not filter out.

A lot of the information pouring in from our surroundings may seem irrelevant, but there's a chance that since we then have a lot more information to work with, we may be able to make connections between previously unrelated ideas to solve problems in surprising ways. When scientists purposely disturb the brain's filtering mechanisms, people become more imaginative and insightful as problem solvers. The fact that we notice details that seem completely unconnected at that moment may give us more resources to work with when facing a challenge.

Creativity

When you think of creativity, you probably think of the arts, but creative thinking can show up in almost anything that we do, from doing our math homework, to solving the eighth level of that new videogame, to devising a way to reattach the bumper to the front of your car so that you won't have to pay to get it fixed. Have you ever gotten intrigued by a physics problem and devised your own way of approaching it, only to be given a lower grade by the TA because you didn't follow the right process? Some of your courses won't encourage or reward your creative thinking, and instead will encourage you to stay in line and follow the rules, but our creative potential is part of what makes us unique. Once we recognize this, we can learn to put our unique wiring and creative potential to good use.

True creativity doesn't follow a straight line and it doesn't color between the lines. Society tells you that you need to do things a certain way: go to school, take these courses, get these grades, graduate and get a certain kind of job. But creative people don't always stick to the designated pathway to success. They often take detours, they double back, and sometimes they wipe the slate clean and start over completely. They feel compelled to find their own way.

Billionaire entrepreneur Sir Richard Branson is a known risk-taker who earned his fortune not in spite of, but precisely *because of* the traits associated with his ADHD. He stepped off the beaten path when he dropped out of school to put his creativity to good use. He started his first business, Student Magazine, at age 16. Now, he is one of the most famous entrepreneurs in the world and the founder of Virgin Group, a group of over 400 enterprises including Virgin Records, Virgin Airlines and Virgin Galactic. He goes beyond just taking really big monetary risks in starting new businesses; he also promotes his businesses with dare-devil stunts that most people would think are crazy. He has even crossed the Atlantic in a hot air balloon and driven a tank through Times Square to promote his businesses.

But perhaps even more impressive than his willingness to risk it all in business, is his commitment to exploring his seemingly endless creativity. He finds inspiration in his frustrations and uses them as the catalyst for his creative process. Can't get the flight you want? Start your own airline! Literally. A frustrating experience in an airport led him to launch Virgin Airlines when he had absolutely zero experience in the field. When there is a problem that needs solving, he channels his energy into figuring out a new and unique way of doing things, creating business after business, and opportunities beyond belief.

If you thought that ADHD could only sabotage your attempts at success and limit your possibilities, think again. Just take a minute to let this sink in: Branson founded Virgin Galactic because he wants to take *regular people* on commercial flights into *space*. To him, there seem to be no limits whatsoever. It's true, some of Branson's risky behaviors have gotten him arrested. But his willingness to take risks, combined with his potent creativity has earned him an international business empire and a private island to call home.

Procrastination

You are probably already asking how in the world procrastination can be viewed as an advantageous trait. Waiting until the last minute to get to work on a task is classic ADHD. We will push things off for as long as humanly possible, typically making things into an emergency situation before we realize that there is no way to push off that project, paper, or presentation any longer. For example, let's say you get a parking ticket, but then put off paying it for weeks and weeks. You just aren't motivated to shell out that $20 until you find out that they won't let you register for your next semester's classes if you don't pay up. So, now that the last day for course registration is upon you and the situation is urgent, you get the ticket paid, and finally get to sign up for your courses. This experience is all too familiar to us.

Obviously, one of the problems with this is that sometimes we wait too long, and then we can't quite pull things off the way we had hoped. But, I'm sure that you also know the flip side. Once you've created a crisis of epic proportions, adrenaline kicks in and your brain finally gets the stimulation it was striving for. This lets you channel your energy and focus to get your work done. It's hard to picture how procrastination could possibly be connected to survival.

Procrastination may be one route to your highest creative potential. As you procrastinate, your brain is busy running processes in the background, exploring paths, making connections that you aren't even aware of in your conscious mind.

However, the connection to your genetic inheritance is still there. Hunters were successful when they could act quickly and decisively in dangerous situations with high pressure and life-or-death consequences. Our brains know that we can perform well under pressure, and so we try our very best to duplicate the feelings of this dangerous environment in our daily lives. Through procrastination, you create a crisis that then helps you turn on the brain chemicals for focus, get in the zone, and perform at your best.

Because our brains are wired to perform optimally under intensely stimulating circumstances, we may actually *need* to procrastinate on our projects to get them done well. If you start the project too early, your brain may not have the chemical stimulation it needs to move into the ultra-focused state. You will most likely find yourself distracted, and wasting time doing other, more enjoyable, things anyhow. When you wait until four in the morning to start writing that lab report due at your 8 o'clock class, you are creating what feels like a life-or-death scenario. If you don't hand it in, you risk failing your course. Your internal alarm bells are ringing like crazy, and your adrenaline kicks in. This puts your brain on high alert, and your thoughts zero in on your task with the laser-like precision that finally lets you get your work done.

Typically, people will tell us that the best way to avoid stress at school is to stop procrastinating. They will offer tips on how to stop your bad study habits and how to break work down into small, manageable chunks that it will fit into your daily schedule. That might work for some people, and if it works for you, then by all means, do it! But understanding how your brain works at least allows you the possibility to embrace your procrastination and fine-tune it. Make it work for you. You can observe yourself and find the sweet spot: that moment when you have just put your brain into high gear, but you haven't waited so long that your task is impossible. This way, you can do your best work in a limited amount of time.

Beyond this, I'm going to offer you another viewpoint that you might not have considered: procrastination may be just one very indirect route to your highest creative potential. As you procrastinate by doing other things than what you are *supposed* to be working on, your brain is busy running processes in the background, exploring paths, making connections that you aren't even aware of in your conscious mind. Leonardo Da Vinci, one of the most celebrated artistic and mechanical geniuses in history, was known for his tendency to get bored quickly and got distracted easily when he was not engaged in creative projects. He was also, perhaps, one of the most extreme procrastinators in recorded history.

Da Vinci once wrote that, "Men of lofty genius sometimes accomplish the most when they work least, for their minds are occupied with their ideas and the perfection of their conceptions, to which they afterwards give form." In other words, while you are procrastinating, your brain is busy playing with concepts and weaving a surprising web of interconnected ideas. Da Vinci took 16 years to paint the Mona Lisa, putting off those finishing strokes until he had mastered every angle, every shade, and every flash of light. Works of genius take time to perfect. Masterpieces can't be scheduled according to a rigid timeline. What if procrastination is an integral part of the creative process? Consider, for just a moment, the possibility that what your teachers and parents may have called "slacking off" is your brain's way of incubating the seed of an idea and exploring all the possibilities so that you can invent, create, and innovate.

Scanning

Almost every book about ADHD starts out by talking about "inattention." We probably all received report cards in middle and high school that pointed out how we always seemed "distracted" or "off-task" in class. This probably wasn't entirely true. We *were* paying attention, just not to the lesson. We were scanning our environment for something more interesting in the world outside the window. Notice the mismatch between your ability to notice everything at once, and the school's expectation that you pay attention to only one particular thing at a time.

Your mind's "distracted" behavior can play a key role in creativity. The things that would seem totally irrelevant to typical brains just might be the catalyst that helps you make an unexpected connection or take the next leap forward in science, in business, or in whatever field you choose to pursue.

You are supposed to be listening to your professor explain how to follow the prescribed steps to solve a boring chemical equilibrium problem. Instead, your eyes and ears are all over the place. You are noticing the extremely loud buzzing sound in the air conditioning system. You've even started writing and illustrating a comic about the tiny fly that is trapped between the screen and the window pane and its heroic rescue by a gentle giant spider. Moving on, you attempt to draw an intricate portrait of your professor, making sure to feature the extremely long hair growing out of his right ear. If our classes don't light up that dopamine pathway, then our brains are going to be looking for something more stimulating to think about. As hunters, we would be scanning the forest for noises and movement, aware at every second of each possible danger, and each potential prey. Your scanning ability would make you more likely to come home with some food for the evening's meal than someone who was so focused on staring into the clearing that they missed the quiet deer nibbling on acorns deep in the woods in their peripheral vision.

We can learn to use this scanning ability to your advantage. You can think about your brain like a computer's GPU (Graphics Processing Unit). A traditional CPU (Central Processing Unit) is made up of a few cores that can perform sequential serial processes. This is similar to a typical brain that is able to think linearly and focus deeply on one task at a time. In contrast, a GPU has thousands of smaller cores that provide great processing power. Your brain's ability to pay attention to everything at once makes you able to focus your intense processing capacity on the problems that are most interesting to you. This provides the environment for the divergent thinking that is so critical for creative problem solving. When you notice more things, you have more information to draw from and more ideas to connect in your creative endeavors. On top of that, the brain's capacity to solve problems through non-linear thinking by making rapid-fire connections between unassociated ideas can lead to new insights.

The seemingly random questions that fill your head can lead to intriguing possibilities. For instance, you may find yourself wondering what would happen if you used that magnet from the white board on the substance that you are working with in the chemistry lab. That's not the question that you are supposed to be working on, but you do it anyway, and notice that something strange happens. You discover that this new knowledge can be used to develop a material with unique properties. Do you see how sometimes a random thought can lead to a surprising and exciting discovery? Sometimes, these unexpected developments that arise from seemingly random associations are key in the development of new and innovative technologies.

Innovation happens when someone manages to make connections between things that seem unrelated. Your mind's "distracted" behavior, just like procrastination, can play a key role in creativity. The things that would seem totally irrelevant to typical brains just might be the catalyst that helps you make an unexpected connection or take that next leap forward in science, in business, or in whatever field you choose to pursue.

Hyperfocus

This is probably one of the less frequently mentioned ADHD traits and it is connected to your brain's hunger for dopamine. Dopamine is sort of like a doggy biscuit for your brain. If you teach your puppy to shake hands and roll over three times, all while howling the happy birthday song, and then you give him a treat, he will keep on doing it over and over because he wants the cookie. When we find something that triggers a dopamine reward in the brain, we want to keep it going for as long as possible.

This mechanism may be what gives us the unique ability to focus on an enjoyable activity without stopping, possibly for hours on end. For many of us, it is videogames. For others, it may be working on a complicated art project or assembling the parts of a remote-controlled cat-shaped robot for your fluffy white kitten to play with while you are in class. I am sure that you already know that there are some things you can do for hours. Of course, the down side to your ability to focus exclusively on one very enjoyable activity is that all the other things that should be on your to-do list fade away behind the backdrop of your intense engagement. Your brain kicks into overdrive and produces that enjoyable rush that keeps you plugged into your task.

If you were (or still are) one of those kids that would play videogames for six hours straight, not even pausing to eat, drink, or go to the bathroom, you are probably familiar with this sensation. Everything else disappears. It is just you versus the zombies for hours and hours. Any interruption that breaks the positive feedback loop is an unwelcome and painful experience. When you stop, the world comes flooding back in. You realize that you are hungry, thirsty, it's super late, you haven't even started your homework, and you *really* need to go to the bathroom.

The ADHD brain kicks into high gear when it is highly interested. This hyperfocus would have been (and still is, for some) essential for hunters on the chase, or fighters engaged in combat on the war front. We have been told that we can't pay attention for long periods of time, but that's not even remotely true. We are actually capable of paying attention *more* intensely than a lot of people, but only if it is on something that rewards us with extra dopamine because we find it interesting. My students with ADHD can work for long hours on engineering research projects, as long as they are personally interested in and motivated by what they are doing. This is one way that you can start to work with your strengths. You are going to be most productive when you have a say in what you are doing, and you are following your passions. Yes, you will need to take some prerequisites or general education classes that may bore you to tears. But once you learn how your brain responds, and what flicks the switch on to overdrive, you may be able to find more ways to incorporate this ability into more of your classes.

How can we use our self-knowledge to flick the switch that activates our innate ability to hyperfocus? Maybe you are an art major, and you've always loved to illustrate stories or draw comics. In fact, you often get so sucked into your creative work that you have skipped countless meals by accident. Still, you are having a tough time feeling engaged in your English poetry course. You keep trying to do the reading, but instead, you find yourself waking up with your cheek smashed into a puddle of drool on top of your Norton Anthology of English Literature. How will you possibly find the focus that you need to get engaged with this topic? Can you find a way to bring in your passion for art? Maybe you can illustrate your understanding of the important poems by painting the key images or by turning the verses into a graphic novel.

If you take the time to build a good relationship and establish communication with your professors, you may even find that some of them may be willing to accept your creative work as an alternative or a supplement to an essay or presentation. If not, at least you have found a more enjoyable way to study for your English exam. If you can easily enjoy spending four hours drawing a comic about something, you are cementing your understanding of the material in your brain with funny visualizations that make it easier to remember. Figuring out ways to switch on your hyperfocus in a variety of situations can allow you to take advantage of your natural strengths to become more productive and learn more easily.

Boundless Energy

If you've got the high energy and increased physical activity associated with the "H" in ADHD, then you know how hard sitting still in a boring class can be. The traditional classroom can be one of the least friendly environments for highly active people. In the past, increased physical and mental activity most likely contributed to higher success in hunting and foraging activities, and probably helped people to defend themselves from threats. The highly active members of a hunter-gatherer society might cover more ground when gathering food or hunting wild game and would be better nourished as a result. They might also be more successful in fighting off the large predators that they encountered in the forest.

So, how does this help us now? There are plenty of ways that we can capitalize on our high energy level. Maybe you're an athlete, actor, performer, or dancer. Justin Timberlake, singer, dancer, and actor, has both ADHD and OCD. Karina Smirnoff, of *Dancing with the Stars*, has ADHD, too. Lisa Ling, journalist, actress and television host, was diagnosed as an adult! Professional athletic leagues and Olympic teams are loaded with people who have ADHD traits. We've mentioned Michael Phelps, already. Simone Biles, the gymnast who won 4 gold medals in the Olympics in Rio de Janeiro, made headlines when she publicly announced that "ADHD is nothing to be ashamed of" after hackers tried to discredit her by publicly posting information about her medication.

But even if you aren't a performer or an athlete, you can still draw on your boundless energy for success in your career. Many professions offer huge financial rewards to people with the high energy levels associated with ADHD. If you can hustle all day, buzzing from customer to customer, enthusiastically making the pitch that is going make a deal happen, you can make a killing as a salesperson. Our ability and willingness to do the unexpected can give us both the unusual ideas for successful entrepreneurship, and the guts to make it happen. Add high energy to the mix, and you've got just what is needed to work 18 hours a day for two years, sell your startup company for $500 million, and then move on to the next big idea.

For John T. Chambers, Cisco's former CEO, ADHD and dyslexia are integral parts of the out-of-the-box thinking style that helped him achieve huge success as an entrepreneur. Always ahead of the curve, Chambers pushed his high energy into pursuing the next big thing, turning a simple router business into a massive IT company that was running models of an Internet-connected refrigerator years before the Internet of Things was even "a thing." To keep up with the breakneck speed of technology, Chambers leveraged his ADHD to keep his company moving forward.

Risk-taking

If your parents had to install locks on the top part of the doors so that you wouldn't run out into the street when you were a toddler, or if they regularly found you swaying in the wind at the very top of a 100-foot-tall tree, you know all about risk. From drinking and then driving home with a person you have never met before, to jumping down a flight of stairs just to see if you can make it, risk-taking runs across a whole range of behaviors, some of which can, obviously, kill you. As a member of a hunter-gatherer society, you would have had to risk your life daily in your attempts to kill dangerous large animals for meat. Having a small number of risk-takers in society lets a few people take the necessary risks to survive (dangerous hunting expeditions), while the majority who stayed at home would benefit from the bounty of the hunt. Unfortunately, this ability is generally not appreciated in the same way in our modern, industrialized society.

Even though most schools regularly punish us for risk-taking behaviors, the fact is that risk-taking isn't always bad.

In some cases, there is a tremendous payoff for pushing the envelope. CEOs and entrepreneurs routinely put their money on the line when they start a business. Would you risk it all to start a business that you believed in with all your heart? Would you risk your professional reputation to pursue a line of research that makes most people think you are crazy?

I was told by some that investigating the connection between ADHD and creativity in engineering education programs would be a distraction. It was a huge risk to follow my passions and step outside of the prescribed, traditional research areas expected of me. But I did it, and the support from the National Science Foundation, as well as the feedback that I have received from students and families, has encouraged me to continue. I still believe that what my students and I uncover in this research has the power to change things for individuals, for families, and for our nation. In research, it is the willingness to do the unexpected that pushes us forward out of stagnancy and into the space where creativity can thrive.

Impulsivity

Impulsivity is what allows us to make snap decisions. In a fast-paced, high-risk environment, this is an advantage. It would give us the ability to do things like jump from a runaway horse before it gallops straight into a ravine. This same impulsiveness would have allowed the deer hunter to drop everything and suddenly veer off course in favor of following bear tracks. In a less intense environment, this is not always an advantage. We do things sometimes without thinking about the consequences. Whether your impulses tell you to shove peas as far as you can up your nostrils during a lunch meeting with your professor, to see how fast you can get your car up to 100 miles per hour while driving across campus, or to go cliff diving in the quarry by yourself at night during a thunderstorm, this trait can result in consequences that range from mildly embarrassing to devastating. I'm sure you may already have some experience with this.

But this impulsivity might also be described as spontaneity or flexibility. Yes, you might sometimes do things that logic cannot possibly explain, even in an eleven-dimensional universe described by string theory. This ability to quickly change course or to pursue a sudden opportunity without overthinking it can lead to some fantastic opportunities.

Imagine that your professor mentioned that she had a position open up unexpectedly for a research assistant on her trip to Costa Rica. Would you jump at the chance, even though you didn't know how to speak Spanish and had never left the country before? If you would only drop by for an interview that very afternoon, you'd have a chance to be hired right away. A less impulsive person would probably not jump at the chance before evaluating all possible consequences and might miss out on the opportunity of a lifetime. Under the right circumstances, the willingness to make a snap decision can be just the trait that you need to make something amazing happen.

Emotions play an integral role in all our mental processes, our impulses, and our decision-making. Since ADHD can make our highs and lows seem extreme, many of our thought processes and decisions can seem extreme, as well. Because the intensity of these emotions can make us fixate on them to the exclusion of anything else, we can feel like our brain has been completely taken over by something that most people would see as a minor issue. When we are pumped about something, we go all in. When we get rejected, it can feel like the apocalypse. When we are frustrated, sometimes we get so overwhelmed by negativity that we just shut down. At these times, things can feel so intensely challenging that it is easy to get completely discouraged. However, these intense emotional reactions to difficult situations don't have to lead to self-destructive actions. Frustrations can be a powerful driving force for creativity.

Don't be afraid of your intensity, and don't fear following the unconventional path that it may lead you down. Take your emotions and learn about them, take your frustrations and use them as a catalyst, and take your crazy ideas and figure out which ones of them just might be worth the risk.

Remember the example of Sir Richard Branson? He started his own airline just because of an occasion when he couldn't get on the flight that he wanted. He was so intensely aggravated by his negative experience with what he felt was a sub-par airline that he went to the extreme of exploring how he could perfect every single detail of an airline, right down to the creation of a more entertaining safety video at the start of a flight. When you have such a negative experience that you want to make a change, you have the catalyst for innovation. Without intense emotions, it is easy to fall into complacency. Even if something negative were to happen, you might not care enough to do anything about it. But if the experience impacts you deeply, or offends you to your core, it is almost as if you feel compelled to do something about it. Our intense emotional responses can lead us to take transformative actions.

When we allow our emotions to drive our actions, we can find ourselves following truly unconventional routes, making decisions that no one can possibly understand from a "rational" perspective. As a student in Iran, I was on course for what would seem to be a successful life. I had made it through an extremely competitive admissions process and claimed one of the few spots at a prestigious university for PhD students. I had completed almost all the challenging coursework and was *this close* to finishing my degree. I had a good job, a nice house, and a good marriage. All I had to do was keep following this course. My life was pretty much all set. But of course, in grad school, things don't go perfectly. There are always going to be problems with the lab, or you will have moments of frustration with your research or conflicts with others.

When I was younger, these frustrations swelled like a tsunami that threatened everything in its path. Eventually, I became overwhelmed by the tidal wave of dissatisfaction, and something had to change. So, I did what pretty much no one else would do in this kind of situation: I quit my PhD program without finishing, sold the nice house, and moved half-way around the world to start all over with a new PhD program in Nevada while living in a tiny, run-down rental housing unit for graduate students. All my traits: the impulsivity, the intense emotions, the risk-taking, combined to form a perfect storm that took me on a journey that I could never have predicted.

To most people, I was crazy. Who would give up everything, only to start from scratch on the other side of the world? Yet here I am, living a life that is, by most definitions, successful and pursuing research that is deeply rewarding. Once we learn about ourselves and our intense emotions we may be able to learn how they can work for us and against us. Even though sometimes, this emotional intensity will lead us to do things that we may regret, other times it can open unexpected doors that most people would be too afraid to step through. For me, these emotions ultimately led me to cross the globe and helped me to step outside of the "normal" engineering research box to explore how ADHD can drive creativity and innovation.

So, don't be afraid of your intensity, and don't fear following the unconventional path that it may lead you down. Take your emotions and learn about them, take your frustrations and use them as a catalyst, and take your crazy ideas and figure out which ones of them just might be worth the risk. Get to know your high energy, your risk-taking, and your impulsiveness, and use them to fuel your creative fire. Who knows? You might be the next one to change the world.

- 4 -

THE LEARNING PROCESS

Now that you are in college, you may find yourself wondering why you are required to spend so much time completing the numerous general education requirements mandated by your college. Is Drawing Fundamentals just a distraction from your Biology focus? Are you wasting your time and money by taking that writing-intensive freshman English seminar, when you'd really rather be spending your time learning about circuits and sensors? The poor delivery of course material and biased evaluation methods of many of these courses can make it tough for us to see general education courses for what they can be: an opportunity to expand our abilities, knowledge, and skills through a diverse learning experience. How can we take ownership of our education in such an imperfect system? By leveraging our innate curiosity and bringing our unique passions and abilities to the table, we can find joy in our own learning process. Ultimately, this may enrich our lives and increase our already powerful potential for creativity.

Diversifying

Leonardo Da Vinci had hardly any formal schooling whatsoever, and yet he is still considered one of the most extraordinary minds in history. Perhaps because of his informal education, he was able to follow his pursuit of knowledge in whatever direction he desired, and he considered himself an expert in everything from engineering and architecture to sculpture and painting. He studied the human body through the dissection of cadavers, examined fossils, designed flying machines, learned about botany, engineered bridges and weapons of war, and obsessed about the flow of water as it swirled in rivers. His ability to make connections between diverse areas of study is part of what made his work so outstanding. Da Vinci's mastery in one field often pulled from his knowledge of another. For example, his sketches of *The Last Supper* included detailed drawings of precise geometric forms, and the accuracy of his paintings of the human body depended on the extensive knowledge of anatomy that he gained through the examination of corpses. Da Vinci's artistic ability combined with his great understanding of the sciences to elevate his work to a supreme level of achievement. So how does this relate to you and your college experience?

We so often think that to become a master at one thing, we must focus on it exclusively. Many students today perceive general education courses as an expensive waste of time that just distract them from their major. In fact, these courses that you may perceive as irrelevant are not there to punish you, even though you might feel like it. These courses are there to enhance your understanding and experience so that you have a broader base of knowledge to pull from in your field of study, and more ways to make connections between fields.

For example, you may think that studying a second language is impractical since you want to be a structural engineer. However, when you consider the importance of globalization in today's world, you may see that speaking a second language can actually expand and enrich your opportunities. So many of today's companies are international and so many projects are not contained by national borderlines. Once you get a job at that engineering firm, your ability to speak a second language might help you to be chosen for the team tackling the international projects. Taking time to study a second language and culture can, in fact, be a way to add value to whatever else you are studying because it broadens your perspectives and allows you to consider your ideas from multiple angles.

Perhaps you are studying electrical engineering and are required to take a psychology course. Is this a waste of time? Not necessarily. As you increase your understanding of how people work and think, you add to your ability to connect with people in different ways and navigate the complex world of work, business, and career. These general education requirements can add to your abilities and knowledge, helping you to become a well-rounded person with a more diverse skill set.

It might help to think of it this way: our brains are already dedicated to entertaining multiple trains of thought at the same time, often jumping rapidly from one thought to another and making unexpected connections between different concepts. This is one of the things that helps us to be more creative. When we learn multiple subjects through general education courses, we are unknowingly mirroring this internal process, providing our brains with all kinds of different material to utilize in our creative work.

By diversifying our studies, we may ultimately be able to create something that is more useful to society. Da Vinci reached greatness by studying just about everything under the sun. In the same way, art majors may find a greater depth in their work when they understand mathematics, and engineering majors may find a deeper significance to their design decisions when they have a broader understanding of social issues. Steve Jobs created computers and smart phones that are so successful because he knew the importance of both engineering and design.

As Jobs, himself, said:

> *A lot of people in our* industry *haven't had very diverse experiences. So, they don't have enough dots to connect, and they end up with very linear solutions without a broad perspective on the problem. The broader one's understanding of the human experience, the better design we will have.*

> *Wired, February 1996*

Problematic Presentation

We know, then, that our general education requirements can be part of the material woven into the fabric of our creative work in our field of concentration. But for us, there may be many barriers within the education system that may get in the way of our curiosity, motivation, and learning process. Of course, these roadblocks can feel daunting to us, since our dopamine pathways function differently than most people. This can make it even more challenging for us to feel motivated and to stay engaged in our classes.

One of the most obvious roadblocks for us, is that while the subject material itself may be enriching and important for us in becoming well-rounded individuals, many courses are presented in the most unpleasant way by professors who can be dead boring. The subject itself is not truly the problem. Almost anything can be interesting if presented in an engaging way! Whether it is the varying uses of different types of concrete or the life cycle of nematodes, a good teacher can bring any topic to life. But the monotonous recitation of black and white text projected on slides in a dimly lit classroom is enough to leave anyone uninspired.

Have you ever started out a class with all the good intentions to stay engaged in the lecture and take your best notes, but then drifted off into your imagination instead? Within minutes, you find yourself imagining a circus troupe of lemmings performing acrobatics on a trampoline while wearing tutus instead of outlining the stages of child development. Poor presentation of any subject can lock both educators and learners into a linear, point-by-point thinking pattern that can leave little room for creativity or discussion, marginalize the learning needs of nonlinear thinkers, and force students to become passive members within the education process.

If students are expected to come to class as an empty container, conform their thoughts to a prescribed set of bullet points, and let the slides dribble tiny bits of information into their notebooks, how will they be able to actively engage in the learning process? Some professors will give you no opportunity to ask questions, and if you do, they may seem trapped by the content of their prepared lecture and unable to deviate from their planned remarks. What is the point of this? They may as well have just printed out the slides and emailed them to you to read on your own time.

On top of the questionable presentation of the course material, many courses then evaluate students through exams that emphasize rote memorization of lists of facts. For those of us who may have difficulties with working memory, we may feel like the deck is stacked against us, and it is. This kind of evaluation can be a barrier to our success, since it is not designed to allow us to show our strengths. The entire education process can feel lifeless and utterly devoid of creativity. Still, we are required to participate in these courses, even though they may leave us feeling unengaged, uninspired, and unmotivated.

So, what, then can we do about it? It seems that the first option is to find a way to be successful at these things that do not come naturally to us. That is why so many books focus on trying to provide strategies that will allow you to mold yourself into a "typical" student who can easily take notes, pay attention in your classes, and then study from flashcards. Some of these strategies may work for you, but it also may help to think about the bigger picture. The education system is flawed and can leave you feeling left out of the learning process. It is time to rethink your entire learning process from start to finish. How do you learn? What gets you excited? How can you put the joy back into these classes that may leave you feeling so discouraged?

Joy of Learning

My experiences as both a student and an educator have shown me how easy it is for the joy to be squeezed out of education. When I was in school, I hated some of the engineering courses that focused so very much on memorization. These were the classes where I felt like the life was sucked out of me in a cascade of soulless questioning: name 5 toxic chemicals that may be found in rivers in industrial regions, or, follow such and such a formula to find the traffic demand of such and such a road. The facts were disembodied from the greater context and seemed meaningless because of it. It is too easy for professors to get stuck in a rut of formulaic teaching that makes it hard for students to embrace the learning process.

But it doesn't need to be like this. **Learning is a joyful process.** Intuitively, we all know this. When you are learning something that you are truly interested in, you are full of life and energy. This is that spark that sets your brain on fire and gets you engaged for hours. Our challenge, as learners with ADHD, is that we must find a way to light that spark so that we can be engaged with our coursework, even when it is presented poorly.

Studying vs. Learning

Can we actually find our joy within these courses that can feel so punishing? Most of your instructors or teaching assistants will not or cannot accomplish this for you; a true teacher who brings life and passion to the teaching of their subject can be hard to find. They have come through the same system and have the expectations that you will be able to make it through just like everyone else. They will tell you that you need to work on your study skills and tell you how to make flashcards to study from so that you can "pass" the course. Note the words here. The goal is to "pass," not to "learn." And this is part of the problem.

Memorizing a list of disconnected facts might help you pass the test, but it won't help your long-term retention of the information, and it won't help you to learn deeply or joyfully. I know that this probably flies in the face of most of the advice that you have been given over the years, and directly contradicts the books that claim to offer you 10 tips for this or that related to your study habits. The goal typically seems to be to give you a formula that will help you to break your work down into manageable chunks while helping you to find a "system" that works for studying. But since we have atypical brains, typical systems and techniques were not built for us. This means you will have to find your own way, not stick to some tired old formula of how you are supposed to study.

Ask yourself, what is it that you enjoy doing the most? If you can spend hours drawing or painting, then learn economics through drawing and painting. If you love to write comics, then learn Spanish through writing comics. Some people will tell you that you are engaging in a meaningless waste of time. They may not be able to see the connection between the course material and whatever you are doing. But when you get yourself into a hyper-focused state by doing what you love, you are building the connections that your brain needs to learn in a joyful way.

Others may tell us that we should do things a certain way. However, if they do not understand how we think and learn best, then their suggestions will not work for us. When it comes right down to it, your learning process is yours alone. Sometimes we just need to do things our own way, even if it seems inefficient, weird, or crazy to other people.

How can we activate our motivation to learn when the entire structure of the education system seems designed to stifle it? When it comes to motivation, it makes sense to think about dopamine one more time. Dopamine rewards us and helps us to feel motivated. Since we may be less sensitive to the effects of dopamine in our brains, it is harder for us to get and stay motivated. This is why we so often seek the things that flood our brains with dopamine. Think of it as the pleasure principle. We want to do what makes us feel good. So, if your classes are not making you feel good, then how will you get and stay motivated to learn?

This piece may take a bit of self-awareness on our part, which is tricky, since some of us are not always the best at self-observation. We've got to know ourselves well enough to know what motivates us and what makes us stop dead in our tracks. On a very basic level, we might just need a little thing that rewards us for doing something that we don't enjoy: a chocolate, a social media break, or knowing that once you finish your work you can go out and grab a pizza with friends. Just as a nice pen or notebook can help you enjoy taking notes, little rewards can also help motivate you to go to class or get your homework done.

But a deeper motivation may be necessary in the long run, because on top of just going through the motions of attending class and doing your work, you've really got to *want to learn*. And if you are a science major who is being required to take a course that you feel is entirely useless, how will you get yourself to want to learn about it? We can do this by looking for ways to seek pleasure within that course that sounds so tedious. Think about what you love to learn about most, and then find a way to connect it to the class where you struggle.

Play

One way that we can enjoy our classes more is by approaching our studies with the playful mindset that may have gotten squashed out of us in grade school. How many of us have been called out by our teachers because we were found to be doing something that we weren't "supposed" to be doing? Some of us probably spent a fair amount of time in class fiddling around with a spinner or clicker in our pockets, playing solitaire instead of doing our Internet research, or coating our hands with glue, peeling it off in thin, gray layers, and making a huge disgusting gooey ball out of it under our desks. Whatever the distraction may have been, many of us got in trouble in school because we were caught "playing" instead of "working."

In my work with students with ADHD, one thing is clear: play is often a priority. If you were to be a fly on the wall during a creativity exercise that I run with undergraduate engineering students, you would witness an endless flow of humorous ideas, a strong commitment to having fun, and an unstoppable torrent of unusual creations. When given free rein in a room full of tools and materials, along with the simple instructions to "create something that does something," my students with ADHD tackle the project with a playful spirit that unleashes their innate creativity like a force of nature.

Some people might think that leaving a group of students with ADHD in a room by themselves with vague instructions would be a recipe for disaster. How could these students, who so often struggle with getting started on projects, staying motivated, and following through, actually work together productively to accomplish a goal? However, when they are allowed the freedom to play with the resources in their environment and follow their creative impulses as far as they wish, they can and will devote hours and hours to their work, entering a timeless state of hyperfocus created by their deep enjoyment of what they are doing.

It is well-known that play in early childhood is a key component to learning, but as children get older, they are expected to leave their play aside and "get down to work." Recess takes a back seat to direct instruction in grammar and mathematics. The open classroom spaces that give young children the freedom to move and play in preschool give way to classrooms filled with desks and chairs by middle school. By the time students reach college, play is pretty much a foreign concept, and in adulthood, many work environments seem set up to keep people in their cubicles. Some of today's more successful and inventive companies, however, understand that play has an essential place in driving the creativity and out-of-the-box thinking that can lead to innovation.

Google allows their employees to spend up to 20 percent of their paid work time on their personal interests. It might seem counterintuitive to pay your employees to goof off on company time, but pleasure-driven "play" time for employees has led to innovations like Ad-Sense, which as of 2017 was producing a quarter of Google's revenues. By giving people time to experiment with ideas and follow their curiosity, Google has essentially created an atmosphere in which employees feel freed from the rigid constraints of linear thinking, are able to immerse themselves in their creative projects, and ultimately make connections that can lead to innovations in products and services.

Photos of Virgin Produced headquarters (the film and entertainments branch of Branson's Virgin Group) provide another example of a company that seeks to promote innovation through play. Instead of endless rows of gray, carpet-covered cubicles, you'll see comfortable lounges, ping pong tables, bean bag chairs, billiards tables, and a popcorn machine. None of these things sound like they would help people get down to work. Wouldn't it just be a distraction to have all these options for play right around the corner from your desk? But by providing employees with a safe place to engage in play, Virgin Produced is helping their workers break away from the confines of expected behavior and find novel solutions to problems through playful and creative thinking.

As people with ADHD, we are driven to explore and play with our environments, but we so often find ourselves stuck in classes that focus on linear thinking, step-by-step procedures, and rote memorization. Our desire to engage playfully with the subject matter is actively suppressed through poor teaching methods and rigid expectations, which in turn lowers our innate motivation to learn. We need to find ways to think more like these innovative companies, to encourage ourselves to learn playfully, even in the courses that may bore us to tears. By approaching these courses with the playfulness that seems to come so naturally to many of us, we engage our motivation, find pleasure in learning, and release our creativity.

Curiosity

ADHD traits give us an innate, hard-wired drive to constantly scan our environment for new information and explore the world around us. As children, we may be curious to find out what happens if we squash the orange Play Doh into the rug with our fingers, pour finger paint on the floor and roll around in it, or take the TV apart when our parents aren't looking. Our tendency to do surprising things and ask unusual questions in our explorations is one of the first casualties of education, as we are taught that the most important things are to sit still, behave, and be quiet.

Did you ever get in trouble for interrupting your classes with "unrelated" questions? There you were, sitting in your biology class asking the teacher things like, "Are prairie dogs really dogs?" or "What happens if you set a marshmallow on fire?" It most likely seemed like you weren't paying attention to the lesson, and you were probably told to be quiet and stay on task. But these questions, as crazy as they may sound to other people, are a sign that you are engaging with your environment and trying to build connections that may make things even more meaningful to you on your learning path.

Through exploration, we acquire knowledge, and our natural curiosity can be harnessed as a key driving factor in our learning process. This may take some determination, but you already know that you will have to swim against the current to get where you want to go. Look at the course material from all angles and explore it in whatever way makes you light up. Ask questions about everything. What is the purpose of this? Why does this behave like that? I know that many of us have been conditioned to stop asking all the questions that occur to us, and sometimes asking these questions aloud can work against us in the traditional classroom. Not all teachers are flexible enough in their teaching to consider all the unusual ideas that people like us can bring to the table. But you can write them all down, no matter how crazy they sound. You may find something that is a really great question that gets you feeling even more curious about the subject matter. By finding what makes you tick, even in your most boring courses, you can engage your own learning process, and sometimes, you may just discover something valuable along the way.

The future belongs to the curious – don't be afraid to ask questions and see where your curiosity takes you.

- Sir Richard Branson, November 2017

Building Context

When I think back on my own experience as a student, I remember always spending so much more time than my classmates did, reading and rereading the textbook and covering it in underlining. On top of just reading the assigned textbook, I always needed two or three additional references that would help me to fill in the blanks of my understanding. That way, if there was something missing in my class notes, or if something that I had written didn't make sense, I had a backup, because I had taken the time to really investigate things for myself. I reached out beyond the given text so that I could understand things in a deeper, more meaningful way.

My friends were always telling me I didn't need to do it this way. They would ask me why I didn't just do things the easier way, like they did. They didn't seem to expend the same effort that I did to learn things. When I was a student, I didn't have a name for this. Things just worked differently for me than for my peers. Now, I understand that I just have different needs when it comes to my learning process than most people. I also know that this kind of learning difference is not a weakness. Because we think differently, it helps us to consider things from all kinds of different or non-standard viewpoints.

In writing this chapter, I realized that it had been a while since I had been a student myself. How did I approach the task of learning information that was presented in a "standard way?" I had the opportunity to take another look at my own learning process as I began studying for an exam that is part of the process of becoming a U.S. citizen. When people become citizens, they are required to pass a test to show that they have an understanding of the history and government of the United States.

In an effort to help people study for the test, the government prints out a booklet with all of the information that will be included, and they even provide a website where people can print flashcards to study from. Now, some people can get a booklet of 100 questions, print out some flashcards, and learn the information in a couple of hours. But my brain does not enjoy learning in this way. Tell me I need to memorize a bunch of random facts and my brain will start looking for a way out. Next thing I know, I will find myself reading a Wikipedia article about the cast and crew of Shark Tank or some other completely unrelated and *highly* educational topic.

It is not meaningful for me to just learn something to pass a test. For me to be motivated to learn the material, it was important for me to come to a realization: this was not a forced exercise in information storage, but rather, an opportunity for real learning. Reading the booklet was not just a way for me to memorize 100 facts about our country. Reading this book was a chance for me to let my mind meander its way through the history and government of the United States, taking time to really consider the deeper meaning of it all. I needed to read it all, think about the global context of what was happening all around the world during the formation of this country. I needed to let myself get lost on the Internet, reading and thinking about the philosophical and political beliefs of the framers of the Constitution.

Taking the time to just relish the process of learning meant that, yes, it took me about 5 times as long to finish studying as it did for my wife to study the same material. My learning process requires that I take the time necessary to build meaningful context. But the fact that I took ownership of the process also meant that once I got into the material, I enjoyed the heck out of my weekend learning that information. Seriously.

When faced with a potentially boring task, I was able to enjoy it by building context and connections. How does this apply to you as you are facing a long list of course requirements from the university? In this situation, it means that we must work hard to build connections between courses that we might perceive as irrelevant and the things that we love the most. Luckily, this is something that we are good at! Original ideas happen when unrelated things can be combined in new ways. This is the basic understanding of creativity. As highly creative individuals, we can harness our own very strong impulse to make unusual connections. In this way, we can build a network of connections between the required and often poorly presented course material and our passions.

Finding Your Way

You may be thinking that I am telling you that you need to read five books on top of the one that you are already struggling to get through. How could this possibly be helpful to you when you already have a limited amount of time to do your coursework? Does it sound like I am suggesting that you need to just double down on the amount of studying that you are doing? I am not really saying this at all, unless that is how you learn best. What I *am* saying is that when you invest your time and energy into engaging in a joyful learning process using your own passions, you will learn the material deeply the first time around. Since you have taken the initiative to learn the material so thoroughly in a way that utilizes your unique abilities, you may not even need to study quite so much.

When we really engage ourselves in learning by making use of our passions and creativity, we can change even our most hated tasks into something that reflects our unique abilities. In this way, we can experience the excitement that comes with learning and the pure, unadulterated joy of being ourselves.

The point is this: your mind works in its own fantastic way to get you where you need to be, but the education system doesn't usually allow us the space and time that we need to do our learning in the way that we were meant to. You need the freedom to see yourself in each subject. What I mean is that if your passion shines through when you are doing web design and coding, then you must find a way to do this for even your least favorite courses and subjects. Build intricate websites from the ground up about every last detail that you have learned in your organic chemistry class. If you can spend weeks building and rendering virtual 3-D Lego robotic mechs on your laptop, then you must find a way to use these skills and allow your passions to intrude even into that environmental engineering course that is so hard for you to enjoy. This way, you will crave learning the subject because you will be doing what your brain has been telling you to do all along: creating new and unusual ways of seeing things and enjoying the process of learning.

For me, engaging in a joyful learning process means building context by taking the time to learn all the details about something and following the interconnected data trail that brings me from one idea to another. Does this mean that I sometimes spend hours surfing the web, and going off on tangents when I am "supposed" to be doing something else? Yes. But I love it, because I enjoy finding all the pieces and putting them together until I can see the bigger picture. Do not give me a list of facts to memorize without the opportunity to explore the webs that connect them. After exploring the individual parts of the puzzle and finding the connections between them, I feel so much pleasure in seeing the picture that has become clear when I have placed the final piece. If a class denies me the opportunity to explore the meaning of the greater context of the subject, I may lose my motivation to even participate because it is essentially denying me the enjoyment of learning.

When learners shut down in this way because their creative spark is dimmed by an education system that tends to push people into a one-size-fits-all mold, it is truly a tragedy for all of us. We are missing the opportunity to learn and grow in the way that we were meant to because of who we are and how our brains work. In contrast, when we really engage ourselves in learning the material by making use of our passions and creativity, we can change even our most hated tasks into something that reflects our unique abilities. In this way, we can experience the excitement that comes with learning and the pure, unadulterated joy of being ourselves.

- 5 -

STAYING ON TRACK

Everybody wants to give you answers about how to make it through school, how to be more successful, and how to develop good study habits. It would be nice if I could do that, but in fact, this book is not about providing you with a quick fix for the things that are challenging you. Since we are all unique human beings who learn and create in distinct ways, you won't find ten tips for freshman year, and you won't find any checklists at the end of the chapter. I don't believe that any one set of recommendations will always make sense for any two people, no matter how good the advice is.

If I could just make a simple list for you of things to do that would make your life feel easier, then I would just post it on my website and skip writing this book altogether. However, I would like to share with you some of my observations that might help you to navigate the ADHD-related challenges that we can face. Whether our emotions get the best of us, or our forgetfulness leads to unintended consequences, we can feel overwhelmed and frustrated by it all, and can sometimes get completely derailed from our goals. But by becoming more self-aware and building positive habits, we can develop the skills that we need to be more successful.

Life with ADHD can be like rolling a snowball around at the top of a mountain. At any moment, it seems like we can push the snowball just a little bit too far over the edge of the hillside, and then, helplessly stare as it plummets, gathering speed, growing ever larger, until it becomes an avalanche that threatens to destroy the charming village down in the valley. In the same way, when students fail or drop a course, or drop out of school entirely, it generally doesn't happen overnight. It is usually the result of a chain reaction triggered by many small events that take on a life of their own and can no longer be easily managed.

Let me explain this phenomenon using a real-life example. One day you feel run down because you were up late the night before, binge-watching a series or trying to get your reading done. Whatever the circumstances, you find that you just don't feel like completing that homework assignment. Later on that afternoon, since you know you won't have the assignment to hand in, you just can't imagine dragging yourself out of your dorm to go to class. It is so easy to justify it in your head by saying that it is just one time and it won't really make a difference overall, since you know you will easily be able to get the notes from a friend.

For most people, missing just one class might not signal anything particularly important, but for us, this "one time" can really be the beginning of a personal catastrophe from which it is nearly impossible to recover. You have now skipped the one class and you are feeling quite anxious and somewhat ashamed of yourself, and now you can't bring yourself to face the instructor. So, what happens when the next class comes? You skip the class again because you don't want to have to explain yourself and face the wrath of the professor. You find out from a friend that yet another assignment was given during the class, and now you aren't able to hand that in, either. You start to feel overwhelmed by the amount of missing work. The problem becomes more complicated because now you are starting to see your grade drop.

After a couple of weeks of intense anxiety about the situation and now having skipped several classes in a row, you have also failed to hand in your term paper. You can decide to drop the class or settle for a C in the course. If your GPA starts to suffer, you may start to feel that the entire college experience is just too negative, stressful, or discouraging. Do you see how it works? What starts out as just a simple "day off" can quickly become a reason to take a year off from college, which can just as easily lead to not finishing your degree at all. Obviously, I don't want to imply that everyone who drops out of college does it because of a missed class. Life is complex, and there are many other reasons that might cause this same kind of snowball effect.

Still, there is often an underlying process of small, but cascading failures that can lead to huge consequences. The question for you is, once this process gets underway, will you be able to stop it and recover in time to do the necessary damage control and get things together, or is it just important for you to avoid starting the process altogether? Think of it like this: if you are walking through a room full of combustibles, do you stop, lean against the wall, and light up a cigarette? Sure, it's possible that you might be able to get away with missing class or not turning in an assignment every once in a while. Maybe you get yourself right back to class the next day. And maybe you have that smoke without the room blowing up, but honestly, I wouldn't plan on it.

It's almost as if you are sledding down a steep hill, and you don't realize that you're headed for impact with something hard at the bottom. Is there any way to stop when you are half-way down the hill, so that you won't crash head-first into an oak tree? Really, the only way that you safely move forward is to get back out there and do some damage control. If we realize that we are on a dangerous path, take responsibility for our actions, and see what we can do to get back on track, we are going to get a vastly more positive reaction from our professors.

For the sake of this example, we would need to go to the professor, sincerely communicate our awareness of our error, our desire to make amends and commitment to performing better in the future. We would then also need to submit everything that was missing, while accepting that we still may not receive even partial credit for them. Then, without feeling entitled or blaming others for it, we take ownership of the solution and move forward. If we are lucky, we can escape what could be a four-alarm fire with just a minor burn instead of taking down the entire house in a dramatic blaze.

Ideally, however, we get ahead of the situation, and never start the chain of events in the first place. These situations can be like an uncontrolled chemical reaction, with ADHD magnifying everything in ways that you may not be able to predict. If failure is not an option, then we need to think about *everything* as if it were a matter of life or death. We need to find a way to feel the effects of the whole spiral downwards from beginning to end. How are you going to feel if you fail a course all because you took a day off and missed a homework assignment? Anyone can try to explain the logic of the situation, and you most probably already know that there are potential consequences to your actions, but unfortunately logic may not help you to avoid these scenarios.

Many times, we make decisions based on our emotions, so it may be beneficial to activate that emotional circuit in our decision-making process as well. Think about procrastination as an example. It won't change a thing if someone tells us to think logically about the time constraints of our work. The reality is that we won't get started until we start to feel the heat brought on by our emotional reaction to the looming deadline. Part of how we can avoid putting off that paper or skipping that class is to connect the action with the emotion of the consequence. Feel the sinking feeling in your chest, the queasy sensation in your stomach, and the discouragement that you would feel when you face the disappointment of your parents, professors, and most of all, yourself. Then, remembering these sensations, pack your bag and go to class.

Running on Empty

We've talked a lot about procrastination: how it looks, what it feels like, how it can make things pretty dramatic, and why we do it. You may have been surprised to find out that procrastination can sometimes be a good thing, and that you can even learn how to make it work for you. But remember, like all things, it's about finding the right balance between too much and too little so that you don't find yourself in a difficult situation.

If you are anything like me, you can probably relate to the experience of heading out for a drive with only a couple of gallons left in the tank. Imagine that on one particular day, you're on your way to your final exam. You know you need to put some gas in the car, but since the station is just a little bit out of the way and you are already running a bit late, you figure you will just put it off until after the exam. So you start driving, but you don't notice that the gas meter is dropping until a little yellow light on the dashboard catches your eye. Now you're in a bit of a predicament since there's no gas station close by and the temperature outside is starting to drop. What are you going to do? If you run out of gas, you will not only miss your exam, but you will also be stuck on the highway in the freezing cold!

This is where things start to get exciting. You decide that you'll need to stop at a gas station as soon as you can, but you pass exit after exit, and there's not a Shell or a Mobil in sight. Even the car itself seems to be getting anxious as it switches into countdown mode. Out of the corner of your eye, you can now watch an animation of the gas tank slowly draining while a digital display tells you just how many more miles you can drive before the engine will die. You start considering whether or not you should put the car in neutral and coast down the hill to save gas. Things are getting a little intense when, finally, you spot a sign for a gas station. You take the exit and drive as steadily as possible down the road, rolling into the gas station just as the meter turns to zero. A friendly man on the sidewalk helps push your car over to the filling station while you steer the car into place. You've made it, but you it was quite a bit closer than you had intended. Now you're all stressed out and even later for your exam than when you started.

The point is, procrastination isn't always bad, but it certainly can be risky! Imagine the possible scenarios that could result from running out of gas before making it to the station! Sometimes you might make it to your destination without a problem. Other times, you might end up by yourself on a dark country road for three hours while you wait for AAA to show up with a tank of gas. Then on top of that, you fail Organic Chemistry because you missed the final. It's important to keep this balancing act in mind when we think about our procrastination. While we can definitely use it to turn on our brain chemicals and explore the potential of our many creative ideas for our school work, it can also contribute to complicated situations that derail us in ways that we don't expect.

Taking it Personally

When things go wrong, we tend to take them harder than most people because we spend a lot of time focused on our strong emotions. This makes the "little things" feel far worse than they should. The same principle applies to the many rejections, small and large, that we experience in our daily life. We may even perceive some things as signs of rejection, when they really aren't! In other words, sometimes we take things personally, even when they have little or nothing to do with us.

This tendency to take things personally can have a large effect on how we act and react to the things that come our way. Do you feel insulted or intensely discouraged when your parents, your boss, or your teacher criticizes your work? If we are unable to draw a distinction between criticism of our work and criticism of our personality, we may mistakenly take it as a personal attack that brings out a disproportionate reaction of negative emotions and disappointment. We may be particularly vulnerable to this misinterpretation because many of us have a long history of being accused by school, family, and friends of either doing or not doing certain things because of our ADHD.

For example, how do you feel if you receive negative feedback about your performance in class or if you receive a lower-than-expected grade on your paper? Do you have a voice running in the back of your head saying, "I'm not good enough. I don't belong here. My professor doesn't even like me. This isn't fair. Is this a punishment?" You may feel this way even though the comments are only intended to help you to learn from your mistakes. You probably won't be able to control or get rid of these feelings. However, if you acknowledge them and are aware of them, you may be able to hold off from taking actions that make the situation worse. That way, you won't end up doing something you regret, like sending an angry email to the professor or the teaching assistant!

You may feel like it is very important that your teachers like you on a personal level. This makes it a bit harder to hear anything that sounds like criticism or disappointment. However, it is important to be able to separate your feelings and perceptions from the professor's judgment of your classroom performance. We really need to take the time to let our emotions pass, and then try to understand what mistakes led to our poor performance. Think it through. Did you have trouble managing your time? Did you not read the questions carefully? Did you interpret the questions in a different way? Was there a tiny mistake in your calculations? Did you put in enough effort studying? None of these problems makes you a less-than-adequate human being. These are all problems that we can address by practicing, studying, and preparing for the next exam. So, instead of taking the criticism as an indication of your character flaws, wait out your emotions, think it out, and make a plan to do better next time. This is all just part of the learning process.

Volcanic Eruptions

Our emotions can simmer like hot magma underneath the surface, just waiting to erupt. These eruptions, when they occur, have the capacity to flood our social, academic, and professional lives with burning rivers of destruction that are nearly impossible to control once they explode. A small, discouraging moment can make us feel so strongly that we need to discharge the pressure by unleashing our emotions on others or by making snap decisions that we may ultimately regret. If your TA gave you only partial credit for an answer on the test, but it is because she did not see the rest of your answer on the back of the page, you may feel intensely angry and frustrated. Trashing her on social media might make you feel better in the moment, but as time passes, you may start feeling that you shouldn't have reacted that harshly. And things may even get worse because now that your tweet is out, you know that you can't take it back. The damage has been done and now you are feeling discouraged and embarrassed.

How can you stop these emotionally-driven impulses from affecting your academic life in a negative way? The strength of our emotions and our ability to fixate on them can make it next to impossible to stop them. I know this from my own experience, and I do not have any intention of saying that you will be able to control the intensity of the feelings that you will be feeling. Still, it is my hope for you that these moments of discouragement, frustration, or anger that you may face do not have to lead to a decision that you will regret.

By observing our emotional responses, we can sometimes reframe our situation, or change the impulses that result from them. Just being aware that the volcano is about to blow its top may help us to evacuate bystanders who stand in the way of harm, or perhaps even redirect the flow of lava to avoid destruction.

When I was a student, I sometimes did things on impulse and then realized afterwards that I shouldn't have done them. For example, I have worked for hours creating a 3-D model for an engineering project and then gotten so frustrated by an error message in the program that I ended up deleting the whole thing. Any logical person could have told me that my action didn't make sense. But reasoning and logic just doesn't make a difference to us if we are immersed in such a strong feeling of frustration. Again, the emotional circuit has overpowered logic and reasoning, so what are we to do when this happens?

One of the things that may help you in this situation sounds almost too simple to be effective: **increasing your awareness of your emotional process.** When you are able to watch your own feelings happening to you, almost as if you were a third person observing, you may be able to realize when your emotions are taking over. This may actually help you to involve your logic circuit a bit more or help you to use strategies that may delay an impulsive response. If you can pause long enough to say, "I am really freaking out right now," or "I'm so mad at my professor right now I can barely even think straight," you might be able to stop long enough to talk to a friend about it. You might talk to your mom before you decide to drop a course or send an email that you might regret. You can get your best friend's opinion before you press "shift delete" and permanently get rid of that paper you've been working on for several hours.

Chances are, by delaying just a bit, you may be able to ride out the really intense feelings without reacting impulsively. You might hear the recommendation that you wait five seconds and move yourself out of the situation. This may help with some things, but five seconds might not always be quite enough for these kinds of feelings. Still, the principle is the same: if you can pause, recognize the emotion that is occurring and then delay a response, you've got a better chance of avoiding negative, impulsive decisions.

One silver lining to these kinds of intense emotions is that they can be short-lived. In the moment that we experience those intense emotions, it may seem that the feeling is going to last forever. That makes the situation even more painful. For example, if one of the papers that I have submitted for publication gets rejected, it may feel demoralizing. Now I know that this feeling is going to pass. If I can ride out my feelings, I will find that I am able to move forward in a more productive way. I might get over my discouragement, try to make modifications, and try submitting my paper to some other journals. By becoming more aware of our emotions, we can sometimes avoid these impulses that can be so destructive.

By thinking about our process of thinking, we are engaging in metacognition. These days, metacognition is a well-recognized and extensively studied process. There are many books and other resources out there that can give you more information about this, if you are interested in learning how it might be helpful to you. I will leave you with this final thought: by observing and thinking about our emotional responses, we can sometimes reframe our situation, or change the impulses that result from them. While we may not be able to stop the volcanic eruption from occurring, we can observe the eruption happening, and take actions to avoid some of the more harmful effects that it may cause. Just being aware that the volcano is about to blow its top may help us to evacuate bystanders who stand in the way of harm, or perhaps even redirect the flow of lava to avoid destruction.

The Professor's Perspective

I must admit that in some rare situations, a poor exam grade is actually the result of a grading error. However, even if this is the case, you should give yourself some time to evaluate your work and come up with a compelling argument, *not an excuse*, and *not an angry rant*, to discuss with your professor. Believe me, sending a harsh email driven by a sudden snap of rage does not help in this situation! I have been on the receiving end of these communications more than once, and I know how intensely it may impact the professor's perceptions of the student's maturity and professionalism. It is deeply damaging when a student sends an email that questions the fairness, intentions, professional conduct, or hard work of the professor. To give you an idea of how offensive it is to receive this kind of message, I'd like to leave you with this example of an actual email that I got from one of my students, in reaction to a homework grade:

"The calculations were an assignment beforehand, what are you talking about? How was I supposed to get that figured in a table after I already made the changes? Not once did i get any indication that a majority of these issues were necessary. I went to your TA office hours asking what the mistakes were, and he refused to answer any question, without a smug "I don't understand the question" response. This is absolutely ridiculous. Your grade makes no sense whatsoever. Explain yourself."

It's All in Your Head

Humans have evolved to perceive nature, the environment, and interactions with other humans in a way that supports their survival. However, it's important to note that our perceptions of these things are not "fact." Rather, our perceptions are shaped by many factors that we carry with us *in our head*, such as our genetics, our upbringing, and any prior joyful or traumatic experiences that we may have gone through in the past. These factors form our beliefs and shape the way we understand the world around us. So, why should we care about this? Because our reactions are driven by our inherently subjective perceptions of our reality.

For those of us with ADHD, this may be more problematic than it is to others, because we tend to let our intense spontaneous emotions define a situation and drive our actions. Our perceptions of an environment or a situation may significantly contribute to our anxiety. I have met with many students who feel impairing anxiety because of a story that they are repeating, over and over, in their mind about a difficult situation or interaction. For example, a few years back, I came to know a brilliant engineering student in her sophomore year. At the time, she was struggling with a paralyzing fear of not being able to get through the semester because she believed that she wasn't *good enough* at one of the classes that was required for the degree. In effect, she had created a narrative in her head that her brain wasn't capable of understanding that subject, that she therefore didn't belong in engineering, and that she wouldn't be able to succeed in college. Despite having gotten A grades in AP-level math and physics classes in high school, and having really enjoyed them, she continued to believe that she just didn't have what it takes to make it through her engineering classes.

I tried to convince her that there was no real reason to be afraid that she would fail the course, but she was so certain about her perceptions that she was considering changing her major. She was so stressed out and anxious all the time that she had no energy left over for studying. She switched her major, but never finished out the semester, and then eventually, she dropped out of school entirely. When I say it was "all in her head," do I mean that it was all imaginary? Not exactly. Her emotions and anxiety were real. Real enough that she left school because the situation had gotten so extremely painful for her. What I do mean is that her anxiety, despite being real *to her*, was not a factual representation of the situation. She absolutely had the ability to be successful in her engineering course, but the negative narrative in her head made things so difficult for her that she chose not to continue in her studies.

We, as human beings, tend to believe that our perceptions and views are facts that are set in stone. However, there is nothing absolute about how we perceive the world, and there is nothing objective about the way we interpret our reality. Our ideas are, quite literally, all in our heads. While this is relevant to some extent for all humans, it may be a bit more extreme for those of us with ADHD because of how our brains are wired. I say all of this to remind us that what we may perceive as an obvious disastrous situation, irreversible event, or catastrophic incident may be nothing more than a set of feelings that can change over time. Our perceptions and anxieties are not fact. Finding a way to understand this distinction may help us to find a way through challenging situations that our brains sometimes create for us.

Groundbreakers

Lest it seem like I am telling you to squash all of these strong emotions that are nearly impossible to keep down, let me clarify a bit. In an educational context, our strong emotions have a huge potential to create situations that we may regret. In a college setting, where our success and well-being depend, to a great extent, on our interactions with our peers and professors, these emotions and our impulsive reactions to them can be a liability. As an undergraduate student, I sometimes challenged professors, and even went to the department head, because I felt so strongly that certain teaching methods were unfair. It is also true that sometimes I paid the price for challenging the status quo; my GPA suffered for it in some instances. But I don't regret taking action because I felt compelled to defend my core values and advocate for what I believed. When your core values are at stake, your intensity can help you fight for what is right. We can use this strength to make change when we sense injustice or when we see something that we know could be made or done better.

As explorers and challengers to the status quo, we have the potential to do the unexpected things that drive societal change. Our strong emotions may in fact be one way that evolution provides us with the motivation to push boundaries and make changes that others might not dare to make. If everyone is busy trying not to rock the boat, then change will never occur.

But some of us are wired to react strongly and act impulsively when we get angry. Put it this way: if a group of rebels hadn't gathered together on a cold winter night in 1773 to throw a massive quantity of tea into Boston Harbor, then the United States, as we know it, might not exist. So, yes, I am telling you that it may be to your advantage to curb those feelings and the subsequent firestorms in the classroom and in your interactions with your professors, since you will almost certainly pay a price for them. But keep the awareness that sometimes, when you get really upset, it may be just the push that you need to get out there and do something that hasn't been done before: start your own company, fight for social change, or find an innovative way to reduce our carbon footprint. Whatever it is that gets you fired up, understand that this fire is part of what gives you the power to break new ground and perhaps make real and lasting change.

Emotional reactions vary from person to person, of course. Not everyone is a bomb waiting to explode. Differences in emotional reactions are typical in people with ADHD, and in fact, cool reactions to important situations can be another manifestation of these differences. Some of us, instead of getting extra fired up by very intense emotions, can show a lack of response to something that should actually deserve a more intense reaction. For example, we may, from time to time, receive feedback from a professor about something important: too many emails that did not receive a response, a missed meeting or two, or slow progress on an assignment. Your professor is giving you an opportunity to improve your performance. This is your chance to make a change for the better.

When we are mindful of our emotional patterns and reactions, we may become more able to navigate them effectively.

But what if your emotional switch just isn't triggered, and you just keep on the way you have been going? What if it doesn't register in your mind that the issue is very important to your academic success? If, in fact, we are underreacting, our cool responses can make our professors think that we are not taking things seriously enough. In this case, we may need to make ourselves feel the emotions of the potential consequences of not reacting strongly to this feedback.

Let yourself imagine the worst-case scenario and feel the emotions that you would feel in this situation. Think through what may happen if you do not make changes to your work or start responding quicker to emails. Will your professor stop taking you seriously because you seem to not care? Will you miss an opportunity to join in on a research project because you seem like you are not interested in doing the necessary work? Will you feel guilty because you have let down your favorite professor? Again, becoming aware of and observing our emotional responses, even when they are cool instead of hot, can help us think through and modify our responses to a situation that can have consequences for us in our academic success. When we are mindful of our emotional patterns and reactions, we may become more able to navigate them effectively.

Dory's Difficulty

You may have seen the movie about a cute little blue fish named Dory who swims the length of the ocean with her friend Nemo in search of her family, even though she can't remember anything at all about them. She often feels that she's swimming against the current in her mission to find her parents despite her problem accessing her memories about them. In fact, it seems that she cannot at any moment trust that she will be able to remember anything at all. I'm giving you this image, because ADHD can make life like this to some extent, and you may not even be aware of it.

These small moments of forgetfulness can sneak up on us. For example, you might think that you will remember your best friend's birthday because it is so obvious and so important to him or her. But the truth is, even though you think you *should* be able to remember something, even very important things can be easily forgotten. You could be sitting in a course that you are super excited about and listening to a really great lecture that leads into an even more interesting class discussion. You are so engaged in the moment that you aren't even taking notes. You are really getting it, and you feel certain that you will be able to remember it later because you are learning so much from the discussion.

The problem is, that even though you are very excited about it, a good portion of the information may not actually be committed to your memory bank. Then, when the day of the test comes, you find yourself drawing a blank. You know you talked about it during that really awesome class, but you just can't remember the details. It might seem like stating the obvious, but taking notes can be your memory's best friend. Here is an insider tip from a professor: we really like students who show their interest and engagement by taking notes.

As basic as it seems, note-taking is a strategy that is important in class, but also in meetings, and in life. So many things may just float on by like driftwood on the tides if you don't manage to catch them somehow. Of course, we all need to find a way to do this that fits our unique style. If you need to take your notes electronically, or using a voice recorder, it still serves the same purpose. If you prefer to hand write your notes, but still struggle with the motivation to do it, you can find a way to make it more enjoyable. Just as young kids like to write with pencils that have fun erasers on top, you can get yourself a nice pen that feels great when you hold it or buy yourself a fancy notebook with gold edges that gets you looking forward to taking down your notes.

Make your notebook your constant companion and note-taking your daily religion. When you are in class, you should take as many notes as possible, so that when the professor casually mentions that very important concept, you know for sure that you'll have access to it later, even if you don't manage to remember it on your own.

I know, some people may have difficulty taking notes. You may have difficulty understanding what the instructor is saying while taking notes, or you may find your mind wandering off into a universe of doodles along the sides of the margins. While this may feel frustrating, and you may find it easier to just get the notes from a friend, I would challenge you to continue the practice of taking your own notes, to the best of your ability, and as frequently as possible. Consciously make an effort to increase your skills in this area. You may find that your ability to take effective notes may improve with time.

While not every idea is a good one, you never know when genius is going to strike, or when an important idea will come to you.

Extremely successful business people, like Bill Gates, are well known for constantly jotting down notes as they go through their day. Even Sir Richard Branson, the previously-mentioned ADHD entrepreneur extraordinaire and founder of Virgin Group, Ltd., goes through tons of notebooks every year. He tries to capture every possible idea that comes to mind or is mentioned in a meeting. He believes that while not every idea is a good one, you never know when genius is going to strike, or an important idea will come to you. You also never know when your professor will say that one thing that really helps you understand the concept in a new way. If you are already taking notes, you'll be sure to have this important thought jotted down in your notebook when you need to remember it later.

Note taking can be helpful in many areas of your life, but you may find that you need additional strategies to help you to remember important dates or things that you need to do. People used to say that you should tie a ribbon around your finger to help you remember what you were supposed to do. But for those of us who have trouble with working memory, this might not even help, since we would most likely look at the ribbon knotted around our finger and wonder what it was even there for in the first place! Of course, now we have all kinds of other ways to remember things: paper planners, desk calendars, and electronic reminders on our computers and smartphones, but even these aren't fail-safe since we can sometimes still forget to use them.

Problems remembering can make things really hard for us sometimes because this leads to all kinds of misunderstandings and complications. If you are talking to your professor about something that needs to be adjusted in your essay, you may tell him that you will do it right after lunch. Then, as you walk away, you may begin thinking about something else, and forget about it altogether. A couple of days later, you may find that you cannot remember all the comments and the changes that the professor requested. Not making a note about this important task that you were supposed to take care of leads to a sense of frustration for you and your professor.

As another example, imagine that your professor has informed your class that there will be a field trip to visit a bridge construction site for your civil engineering course. You are really excited about this, since you have been wanting to do some hands-on work but have never had the chance. You get into a long, complicated conversation about the procedure with your professor, discussing all the technical details of the process while you walk out of the building to your next class. Your mind is swirling with anticipation, and you can't stop thinking about how interesting it will be to finally see, in person, what you have been studying in class.

Unfortunately, you were walking in between buildings when you heard about it, and you didn't stop to put the date and time of the meeting into the calendar on your phone. This means that you never get the electronic reminder from your phone, because you never programmed it in. When you see your professor at the next class, he asks you why you missed the trip. You are completely mortified, quite disappointed, and angry with yourself because you have missed a chance to learn something valuable. This kind of thing happens all the time, and it can make you doubt yourself and your abilities. Likewise, it can hurt your relationships with your instructors, since they may feel that you have let them down, or that you don't care, even when you really do.

Another frequent scenario is having trouble remembering particularly important deadlines or dates. Some of us may suffer from anxiety surrounding important submission dates for applications or other requirements. Whether we are subconsciously avoiding a task because we have associated it with some negative emotion or sensation, or because we simply forget the task, this kind of forgetting can have major consequences that we did not foresee. For instance, think about the deadline for submitting your course registration for the coming semester. You may have been putting off completing your registration because you were anxious about choosing the right courses to meet your graduation requirements. Then, when you finally go onto the school website to select your courses, you find that you have missed the date and now the one course that you really wanted has filled up.

Luckily, there is another section of the course that you can take, but it is with a professor that you've heard is not the best, and it meets only in the morning. This puts you in a tough place, since you prefer afternoon classes and really have a tough time getting up in the morning. Plus, thinking about an entire semester with this particular professor makes you dread going to class. Forgetting the date for class registration led you to sign up for a course section that you didn't really want, at a time of day that doesn't work well for you. That affected your motivation and performance in class, and your GPA overall. We must make our strategies for remembering part of our daily habits, so that we put ourselves in the best position to remember the things that are most important to us.

Long Lines and Traffic Jams

If you are anything like me, you read the title for this section and instantly said, "Ugh! I hate waiting!" We live in a culture that increasingly gives us instant gratification; we can listen to any song we want, when we want it. Now that online streaming services release entire seasons at once, we can easily spend the entire night binge-watching episode after episode of our favorite series. We don't have to wait for the next episode to come out. Waiting patiently can be hard for anyone, but still, some of us have quite a bit more trouble biding our time than others do. We may want everything to happen *right now* and get intensely frustrated when we are forced to wait for something.

You may find yourself swearing when you're stuck behind that one slow truck on the way home and then taking a massively long detour just to avoid driving at 35 mph. You might blurt out your ideas and interrupt others in conversation because you just can't wait until they are done with that sentence. Why can't they just get to the point? You might decide not to get your free flu shot in the student center just because there is a long line; you'd rather risk getting horribly ill than wait in line for 30 minutes. If you'd rather pay $10 to park in the garage than spend five more minutes looking for an empty parking space in the free lot, then you know exactly what I am talking about.

Impatience can rear its head in more subtle ways, too, and some of these things can affect our academic performance. Do you get frustrated when you don't understand something right away? Do you constantly flip forward in the book you are reading just to find out when the chapter is going to end, and then realize that you're spending more time thinking about finishing the text than actually understanding what you are reading? Or do you spend your entire class just waiting for it to be over? Instead of taking notes, you draw an empty bubble for each minute that is left, and then make a game out of watching the second hand as it circles the clock. As each minute passes, you fill in another bubble to celebrate being just that much closer to the end of class. While this can be, no doubt, very amusing, it can also leave you with pretty much no idea of what the class was all about and can lead to you missing an important detail or the announcement of an assignment.

It may be next to impossible to push aside these feelings of impatience, but we can become more aware of them. And this, in turn, can help us to bring ourselves back online when we are checking out during a long class or reading assignment. When we realize that we are feeling impatient for the end of class, we can try to bring ourselves back into the moment by reminding ourselves that, if only for a short time, we need to dedicate ourselves to being fully present. Challenge yourself to engage in what the professor or TA is saying. For example, when you start to tune out, catch yourself and ask a question about what you are learning. Make a game out of your note taking or draw a quick sketch of the key idea being presented. The possibilities are endless, but only you can figure out what truly works to get your brain back on board.

By asking questions or visualizing what you are learning, you are engaging your mind in the process, and this allows you to be present and involved in class. Find a way to be fully committed to the learning process for the hour or so that is your class. It may feel excruciating at first, but by becoming consciously aware of impatience and how it can derail your learning process, you may be able to find ways to trick your brain and consciously get yourself tuned in again. Once you are tuned in, time may seem to fly, and the end of class may arrive before you know it.

Alternate Time Zone

Sometimes it seems like we are running on our very own ADHD time zone. Forget Daylight Savings Time! This is a completely different animal. Many of us stay up very late to get our work done, hang out with friends, hold an epic Street Fighter tournament with some friends in the dorm, start yet another new art project, or to watch *just one more episode* of Game of Thrones. For whatever reason, a lot of us seem to be night owls, and then we have the worst time dragging ourselves out of bed in the morning.

Multiple alarms blazing on and off all morning while you continue to hit snooze? Absolutely. Has your boss noticed your lateness and started to call you up every morning to make sure that you are going to make it to work your shift in the dining hall on time? Do you still arrive late half the time because you get up, but then fall asleep for another 15 minutes on the floor of the shower? Do you then walk across campus in a daze, thinking to yourself, "Why the heck did I sign up for this?" If any of these storylines sound familiar, then you can expect college to be extra challenging as you struggle to manage the details of a daily schedule that seems contrary to your own natural timetable.

If we don't attempt to consciously control our sleep schedule, things can get seriously out of whack, and fairly quickly. The first step is becoming aware of our daily rhythms. When are you most awake? When are you most productive? When do you feel drowsy or feel like you are starting to fade? How does medication (if you take it) affect your feelings of alertness or sleepiness throughout the day? Once you've figured yourself out, try to make the most of your best hours. Schedule your classes accordingly, when possible. If at all feasible, make yourself a sleep schedule, as well, so that you can be more consistent in your sleep patterns. An unregulated sleep pattern can leave students drowsy during class, if they make it to class at all. Obviously, academic performance can be seriously affected by lack of sleep or highly irregular sleep.

It's pretty difficult to control these things, but even small changes can make a difference. For example, if you can cut off your binge-watching after 3 episodes instead of after you've sprinted through the entire 10-episode season, you've managed to give yourself 7 whole hours more to sleep. Some who have difficulty waking in the morning try the dual alarm system, which involves waking briefly to take ADHD medication, and then going back to sleep for a while. That way, it is much easier to get out of bed when the second alarm goes off. Staying aware of where we are with our sleep habits can at the very least give us a fighting chance at making it to our classes, and then staying awake once we are there.

Scheduling

A college schedule can be overwhelming, and the complexity of setting up a weekly routine that meets the needs of your course requirements *and* actually works for you can make things quite tricky. Everyone has a natural rhythm to their energy and ability to focus throughout the day. Are you a night owl or a morning person? Is it hard for you to take two classes back to back? Do you do best when you have a break in between your classes, or does having too much down time throw you off? Be brutally honest with yourself about how you function, and schedule accordingly.

If you are miserable every morning as you try to get yourself out of bed, does it really make sense to schedule an 8:00 am class every Monday, Wednesday, and Friday? Whenever possible, make your schedule work for you!

Things to Do

If you pick up any given book written for people with ADHD, you'll often find a section where they will recommend organizing and prioritizing your tasks by writing out a to-do list. The idea behind this seems sound. We have trouble keeping track of all of the things that we need to do and an equally difficult time figuring out what to do first. So, clearly, making a to-do list should be our go-to solution, right? Maybe. But, then again, maybe not.

Putting things on our to-do list can sometimes feel great. As you add each new item that you need to do, you may get the sense that things are starting to get under control. You may get a feeling of accomplishment just by making the list. You put "Do the laundry!" on your list, and as you write the words, you visualize yourself doing it. It feels good to picture yourself being so productive. Since this is starting to feel nice, you decide to keep adding to your list. First you add "Make your bed!" and then "Read chapter 8 for Chemistry." And then things start taking a turn. Now you are adding anything and everything that you can think of: "Feed the cat," "Do math problems," "Start your final paper," "Take out the trash," and "Vacuum the floor."

Soon your list is two pages long, and you are starting to feel overwhelmed by everything that you have to do. To rectify the situation, you write down, "Take a shower," "Brush your teeth," and "Get dressed." Since you've already done them all, you can check them off right away! Yes! Now it feels like you have really gotten off to a great start. And since you've already accomplished so much, now you can take a break from all of your hard work and spend some time on social media.

As you can see, even this simple act of making a to-do list can get derailed by our brain chemistry. I've noticed this dynamic in relation to emails, as well. Once I flag an email as important, part of my brain seems to think that I have accomplished whatever task I needed to do in relation to the email. On the other hand, if I don't flag my emails as important, I am more likely to stay aware that I need to answer them. So, paradoxically, making to-do lists and marking out important emails that need a response can sometimes trick us into feeling accomplished just because we went through the process of thinking about what needed to be done.

Finding a way to navigate these challenges can be tricky, and it requires some observation and self-awareness to figure out what works and what is just making us feel good. Each of us can figure out the strategies that work the best for us. For example, some people might find that making a point to keep the list no longer than three items could work. Some people can get in the routine of finding their most important email and then answering it right away. My point is that the suggested solutions don't always work in the way that they were intended, and sometimes, we've really got to think about custom-tailoring solutions to fit our unique needs.

Writing assignments can be tricky when you have ADHD. Unless you love writing, this kind of work can often drive us to procrastinate. Even once you get started, it is so easy to get stuck in a quagmire of your own thoughts and feel like you will never wade through all your ideas. You might find it hard to get started on your written work, and then discover that it is even harder to *keep writing* once you have started on your papers. This is a huge issue in college, especially if you are taking writing-intensive courses where the professors hand out writing assignments like candy at Halloween. If that is the case, you may need to develop some techniques to trick your brain into getting started, finding your flow, and keeping at it until you've got a final draft.

Part of unleashing your inner writer is figuring out which part of your brain needs to get activated for you to express your ideas clearly. Professional writers have a lot of rituals: writing at a certain time of day, listening to a certain type of music, writing with a certain pen or pencil, sitting in a certain spot, or even using drawing or other artistic techniques to activate the visual centers of the brain. Finding your own rituals can help you activate your brain's happy place for successful writing.

Of course, as with many of the difficulties that we can face, finding something that works is a highly personalized process that requires self-awareness. What kind of learner are you? Are you a kinesthetic learner who needs to go for a run before writing, or take a dance party break in between paragraphs? Can doodling or painting get your brain stimulated enough to make clear connections between all those ideas swimming around in your head? Does listening to a long set of electronic music get your brain flowing in a different way? If sitting down at a desk and banging out a ten-page essay just isn't working for you, it may be time to think outside of the box to get yourself in the zone.

There are tons of ways to trick yourself into getting through writer's block by activating different parts of the brain. You might have trouble expressing yourself in your own voice but find it easier to write well if you just pretend that you are someone else. Think of someone who is knowledgeable about the topic you are writing about and imagine yourself using their voice. This person can be a writer, an advisor, or even the professor who gave you the assignment. Imagine yourself writing your paper on their behalf and see what comes out onto the page. Experimenting with these kinds of tricks and techniques may help you find ways to bypass your natural tendency to get bogged down in writing assignments and express yourself more creatively.

Teaching to Learn

Your coursework might be getting you down because your professors or TAs haven't perfected the art of teaching, or you might just be struggling to get engaged with a subject because it isn't something in which you have a deep interest. If you are tired of being a passive participant in the education process, one way to challenge this dynamic is by redefining your own role. Instead of visualizing yourself as the student, find a way to play the role of teacher. Have you ever noticed that you learn something very well when you need to present it to the class?

Teaching to learn is not a new idea. Even Seneca, an ancient Roman philosopher said, "When we teach we learn." If you think about it, it makes perfect sense. To be able to clearly communicate information to your audience, you need to understand it backward and forward. You need to organize the information and ideas into clear points, find examples that illuminate the concepts, and figure out the easiest way to help someone else understand the ideas. The concept is fairly simple and straight forward. Put it this way: to teach someone something, you've got to learn it yourself.

There are many ways that you can put this principle into action. You can find a study partner who will act as your student. You will learn the material and find a clear and creative way to present it to your "student." The process of teaching your student will help you to understand what ideas are unclear in your own thinking, and what concepts you need to understand better. If you can't find a study partner, you can certainly find other ways to teach people. You can tutor younger students, or you can design presentations for an imagined audience. You can create a website that presents the information or draw and animate the core concepts that you are learning. You can write a blog about what you are learning. The extra effort that goes into creating something that you intend to share with others translates into real, in-depth learning that you will never get by just sitting passively in a class for three hours a week.

I have observed that many of my own students enjoy the process of sharing their learning with others. In part, I suspect that this is because teaching is inherently a creative process that turns on those parts of the brain that activate joyful learning. Not only are you learning things in your own way, but you are finding unique ways of expressing those ideas to others. By teaching others, you are playing an active, creative role in your own learning, as well.

Social Network

Your social network is one of the most important things to think about as you enter college, but this social network is not about the number of friends you have on social media, or the number of likes that you got on the photo you posted of your raspberry pancakes and *huevos rancheros* from that trendy diner downtown. This is about finding people like us who can affirm that our experience is real, and common, and shared by so many others. By spending time with other students with ADHD, either through friendships or through more formal clubs or groups, we are supporting ourselves through a network of people that know what we are going through because they have been there, too. They know what it's like to feel discouraged by the little things, to be doubted by others, and to internalize the negative messages that we are given as we go through the education system. Just having others around who understand us can make life better!

As people with ADHD, we so often feel alone. We feel like we are the only ones going through the frustrations and the ups and downs. This is why it is also important for us to find and spend time with others who have been through it all, too. It allows us to see ourselves through our shared experiences. This reflection of ourselves helps us to understand that we are not the only ones struggling through the education system. You may have felt like you were going through life on a deserted island and that no one else could possibly ever understand what your life was like. We have all probably felt this way at one time or another, yet when we see each other we feel instantly understood and we realize that we were not the only ones.

Teaming up

Find someone you can trust, such as a sibling, a parent, or a friend who can help you make it to class on time or help you make a color-coded calendar. This person should be someone who can help, without judging you, to target some of the areas that give you difficulty. For example, they could give you a wake-up call in the morning so that you can make it to your job on time. A friend who never misses class might help you out by swinging by to pick you up on the way to class. That way, you won't forget or decide not to go. Team up with someone who can remember the things that you won't remember, who can be detail oriented while you explore the big picture stuff, or someone who finds it easy to help you get your desk and notebooks organized. With this said, however, it is important to remind yourself that by depending on another person to do something, it is easy to become overdependent on them. This can lead to trouble if, for some reason, that person is suddenly unavailable.

Anchors and Allies

For us, personal connections with our professors are one of the keys to our success. We thrive when we know that there are people who understand us, believe in us, and who will challenge us to reach our full potential. If you are lucky, as I was, you may find that *one caring teacher* who can act as an anchor for you when things get a bit choppy. Try to make a conscious and mindful decision to seek out someone who you can trust to give you genuine support, honest feedback, and meaningful advice. A good connection with a mentor can keep you grounded when it feels like things are going off the rails and can also help provide you with the guidance you need to make good decisions, set goals, and find the opportunities that will help you to achieve them.

Sometimes, however, just having one strong connection may not be enough to help us in all of our classes. We need to work hard to connect with our professors and build allies in this often hostile educational environment. This means that we may need to push ourselves out of our comfort zone to build relationships. This can be exquisitely painful, especially if it means that you have to push past your nervousness or anxiety to stay after class, to introduce yourself, and to ask those questions that you had during the lecture. Bring your creative or exciting ideas to the professor's office hours and spend some time talking about your learning style and what gets you really excited. Walk with them back to their office after class to continue a particularly interesting discussion that got cut off by the clock.

When you show your professors that you are truly interested in learning, they are more likely to understand when ADHD gets in the way of you getting your paper in on time or when you miss something important because you got distracted by something completely unrelated. If your professors don't understand your learning and thinking style, they will be more likely to give you lower marks on your homework and quizzes when you approach your physics problems in an unusual way. If they do not see your creative energy, your sense of humor, your unique way of approaching things, and most importantly, your interest and effort, they will most likely just write you off as another lazy student who didn't bother to show up or put in the necessary work.

I'm not saying that we should pass the blame off on others, or on ADHD when we do make mistakes. We still have to accept responsibility for our actions or inactions. Even so, it is much easier to do this when we have taken the time to build a positive relationship with our professors. Without the foundation of our personal connections, it is much easier to withdraw from the harsh judgment of others instead of working proactively toward a solution to our problems. Our professors can be perceived as our adversaries or as our allies. When they get to know you, it is easier for them to look out for you and understand your struggles.

This connection may also help you to stay motivated because you don't want to let your professor down. This is especially important in courses where we have no previous interest in the subject, or in the classes that make us feel the most incompetent. If it is a memorization-heavy subject or something else that emphasizes one of your weaker skills, how will you respond to your inevitable frustrations? Will you simply give up, move on, and drop the course, or settle for a low grade? Or will you make the effort to dig deeper and show your professor that you are struggling but really do want to learn? When they know that you are trying, they will be more likely to help you find a better way to learn the material or give you suggestions to overcome the things that are frustrating you. They may be more agreeable to an unusual request to present your information through a short film clip or an animation instead of a presentation in front of the class or a paper.

We build these relationships, in part, so that our educators will be able to understand the challenges that we are facing. When our professors understand the struggles that we are going through, this may help them to be more accommodating by adjusting their teaching style or their evaluations in ways that are helpful to us and other students. Helping your educators to understand you is a way that you can build a safety net that may catch you when you stumble. If your professors see you as a student who really cares about your work, they will act as an ally to you, even when you have difficulties, because they will truly want to help you succeed.

Final Thoughts

If you ask people like us if they've read any books about ADHD, many of us will say something like, "Well, I started reading it, but I didn't make it past the first couple of chapters." If you've made it this far, then that means that I have done my job. When I set out to write this book, I hoped to write a message to all the students out there who are struggling with those aspects of ADHD that can make college more than just a little extra challenging.

I wanted to challenge you to reconsider what you may have learned about ADHD, and to consider another point of view: that our traits can be used to our advantage in college and in our careers to look at things in new ways, find novel solutions to complex problems, and create in unexpected ways. The mismatch between our wiring and the traditional classroom can cause many difficulties for us. Still, we can grow more aware of how our brains and our emotions drive us to behave in certain ways; we can accept ourselves for who we are, and we can embrace and utilize our strengths.

It is my hope that at the very least, you now know that you are not alone, that you are much more than your mistakes, and that you can stop blaming yourself for the challenges that you face on a daily basis. At the most, I hope that you feel empowered to see yourself in a new way, that you take ownership of your learning process, and that you have gained the understanding that ADHD is not just some unlucky genetic disorder.

You can use your unique potential to create something new and unexpected by embracing your talents, harnessing your high energy, and tapping into your extreme ability to focus on what you love. So, set your goals higher than ever before and move forward with the confidence that you can succeed at whatever you set your mind to.

Now that you understand your genetic inheritance and the special role that people like us can play in human society, you can be free from the negative narrative that threatens to keep you down and feeling bad about yourself. Yes, if you are enrolled in classes in a traditional university setting, you will have to find ways to navigate the difficulties of being a round peg in a square hole. It may be nearly impossible to jam yourself into the role that is expected of you. But now you know that you can create your own space within or outside of the system. You can use your unique potential to create something new and unexpected by embracing your talents, harnessing your high energy, and tapping into your extreme ability to focus on what you love. So, set your goals higher than ever before and move forward with the confidence that you can succeed at whatever you set your mind to. I wish you all the best in college, and beyond.

- 6 -

WALKING THE WIRE:
A MESSAGE TO PARENTS

This chapter is a message to the parents who are reading this book with the hope that it will help you understand how you can best help your student make it through college. The perspective that I am sharing with you here comes from my observations as a professor. I have no instant shortcut or one-size-fits-all solution for you. This chapter is simply an opportunity for me to share my thoughts from an insider's point of view: not only am I a university professor who works closely with lots of students with ADHD and their families, but I am also someone who deeply understands what it is like to live with ADHD in a university setting.

I'd like to address, from an educator's perspective, some of the common pitfalls of parenting a college student with ADHD. My goal is that you will understand the true nature of the challenges imposed on your college student within the university setting, while learning to approach these challenges from a place of balance. It can be easy to fall into a state of denial where you can't admit that ADHD is a real struggle and blame the student for making so many mistakes. On the other hand, it is also all too common for parents to excuse anything and everything because of an ADHD diagnosis.

I would also like to share some thoughts about reaching a place of balance in the struggle between wanting to control the situation and finding a way of letting go so that the student can become an independent adult. These observations are based on my experience working with students at the college level and seeing where they and their families struggled. Finding a middle ground can be difficult, but I hope that you will hear what I have to say with an open mind.

You're Not Alone

I know that some of you may be reading this and feeling like you have a gaping emotional wound in your chest. It would be an oversight to acknowledge the difficulties of the student without mentioning all the struggles that families go through to make it through the school system with a kid who thinks and learns differently than most. The stream of blame, guilt, and anxiety, along with the stress of constantly being judged for your child's perceived failings can be a heavy burden to bear. Just as kids internalize all the negative messages that they receive from the education system and struggle with persistent self-esteem issues, so too, do many parents. If there's one thing I know, seeing your child struggle and seeing them judged negatively can *really hurt*. Even though it may have felt like you were the only ones going through it, you should know that there are large numbers of families exactly like yours who have been living the same reality.

It is this reality, common to so many families, that has led numerous parents to contact me about my research over the past few years. The flood of emails that continues to pour in express the frustrations of seeing a child's unique brilliance become clouded by the rigid expectations of the school environment; it is these emails that have provided me with the greatest motivation to bring this message to students, families, and educators. It is maddening to be told that your child is failing when you are perfectly certain that, in fact, it is the school that is failing your child. I understand what you have been going through. Rest assured, even though you may feel isolated, you are not truly alone.

The stream of blame, guilt, and anxiety, along with the stress of constantly being judged for your child's perceived failings can be a heavy burden to bear. Seeing your child struggle and seeing them judged negatively can really hurt.

These stories that I hear from parents are alike in so many ways. There are so many experiences shared between them all that if I were to stitch them together, it would be hard to tell where one student's story ended, and another began. Invariably, parents will share stories of a student who is uniquely talented in some areas, highly creative, and able to solve challenging problems in novel ways. Then, they will go on to tell me that despite all these strengths, the rigid curriculum, along with the demands of college, have left their child struggling to succeed. They are intensely frustrated with the system, yet they hold out hope that there is something that will work.

It is supremely difficult to face the judgment of others. Your child's classmates and their parents, teachers, administrators, and even your own family members may have been judging you because they just don't truly understand what it means to have ADHD, or to have a child with ADHD. I hope you understand that my intention here is not to judge you, but rather to share my observations with you. Becoming self-aware is so important for all of us: just as the student needs to understand how intense emotions can get them off track, parents also need to be aware of how their emotional reactions and habitual behaviors can have a profound impact on the student.

Fighters

In my conversations with my students, the topic of parental support comes up over and over. I've heard students say things like, "My mom is the reason I'm here," or "My dad forced me to be successful." For many students, this means there was at least one parent who pushed them to succeed, got after them to get their homework done, and fought those battles to help them get their projects and papers in on time. So many of us had parents who fought their heart out for their child or provided just that right balance of understanding and tough love.

Many parents find ways to provide unique or specialized educational experiences, give love and support, and challenge the system to provide what their kids need. You probably know the feeling of walking into your child's high school or middle school for yet another meeting with teachers, administrators, or other assorted school professionals. If you were lucky, you found allies among these professionals: people who believed in your child and went above and beyond to help your child succeed. If you were unlucky, you found yourself in an adversarial situation with teachers who placed the blame at your feet, implied that you were a bad parent, and labeled your child lazy and unmotivated. On top of this, add in the fight for educators to follow through on providing accommodations in the classroom and you've got exhausted parents who all too often end up in conflict with the school system. After waging this battle year after year, many parents become fighters, determined to do anything in their power to help their child succeed. After so many years of battles with the school system, it can be hard for parents to know when it is time to take off the boxing gloves and step out of the ring.

As young adults who must now find their own way in the higher education system, students must build their self-confidence and overcome their fears and anxieties as they also establish healthy interactions with their professors. As parents, you have the unique ability to help your college student acquire the skills they need to take control of their education.

Now that your student is in college, you may feel as if you need to brace yourself for the next fight, and I'm not going to lie to you, getting through college with ADHD can feel impossible at times. The education system at the college level is not designed to support and nurture students with diverse thinking and learning styles. Teaching methods in many courses can be completely inadequate for the needs of students with ADHD, and there may be an ongoing battle with some professors who do not want to or do not know how to provide accommodations or modify their teaching in any way. The fight will most certainly go on, and if you have been the one to duke it out with educators over the years, you may not feel ready to let it go. While this letting go process may be extremely difficult, ultimately, we must find ways to teach students the skills needed to advocate for themselves in the college setting.

As young adults who must now find their own way in the higher education system, students must build their self-confidence and overcome their fears and anxieties as they also establish healthy interactions with their professors. Students may initially find it challenging to manage their education as adults. As parents, you have the unique ability to help your college student acquire the skills to take control of their education.

A New Prescription

When seeking tools that may help students manage life in college, medication is often a subject of conversation. In fact, medication is one of the biggest questions parents have about ADHD. I am not a doctor, but of course I have an opinion. I like to frame the discussion of medication in terms of what you would do if your child had a need for eye glasses. If your child was having trouble seeing what was on the board in the front of the classroom, how would you react? Would you tell your child to just sit at the front of the room so that they could avoid the stigma of wearing glasses, or would you head straight to the ophthalmologist's office for a new prescription? Impaired vision and corrective glasses isn't a perfect metaphor. But if medication can be safe and effective, then it would be a shame to rule it out. Help your student to consider all the options. If your son or daughter feels that medication might be the way to bring the world into better focus, then explore all the possible solutions that may lead to success.

It might also be helpful to know that even medication isn't truly a quick fix or an instant solution. The reality is that many people go through several prescriptions before settling on the right one, and even then, there may be ongoing adjustments to dosage and timing so that the medication is effective. While complicated, the process can be worthwhile, and may be just what your student needs to manage the daily challenges of going to college.

Hovering

If you are one of those fighters who is having trouble getting out of the ring, then you might be in the habit of supervising and double-checking your child's every move. And who can blame you? You are probably thinking that if you hadn't been so heavily involved, that your child would have slipped through the cracks of the education system. You are probably right! So where do we draw the line of doing things for our students and helping them find the way to do things for themselves? Everyone is familiar with the term "helicopter parent." By this, of course, we mean parents who hover over even their college-aged students, watching their every move, and doing anything and everything for them. This is the norm for many college students, whose parents are used to being in constant contact, who have spent years scheduling their every activity, and who most of all, don't want to see their children experience pain, suffering, or failure.

In my experience working with students with ADHD, I have found that some parents have taken their support of the student to the extreme of doing almost everything for them. Throughout the school years, you may have spent years helping your child stay organized, sat alongside them for hours as they did their homework, and provided reminders about upcoming tests or due dates. You may have intervened constantly in your child's education due to conflicts with teachers and advocated endlessly to have your child's needs met by the system. And so, of course, it can be extremely difficult to let the student take over this process when he or she arrives at the university.

For the student, too, this process can be difficult. When students become accustomed to letting others do things for them, they may not even realize what it is that needs to be done. It is very easy for students with ADHD to become over-dependent on family members who have done so much for them over the years. But in the transition to adulthood, it is so important for students to understand that they can take over these processes. They may need some help with learning how, but they must discover how to communicate with their professors, how to register for their classes, how to set goals, make plans, and follow through, and how to manage their time without their parents intervening.

Do you catch yourself texting your kid at all hours of the day to see how they are doing, even when they are in class? Do you constantly check in with them about the due dates of their projects, or whether or not they have been keeping up with their homework assignments? Do you email professors directly about the details of your college student's coursework? If you see yourself in this description, you certainly aren't the only one who has been guilty of hovering! You might be accustomed to being in the pilot's seat, but, as hard and frightening as it may be, it just might be time to take a back seat and let your now adult student take the controls.

I'm not saying that you shouldn't be involved in the process at all. Even adults like to have advice from their parents when things are difficult! But it can make things more complicated for professors when they receive emails from parents about the student's grades or the student's need for certain services. Now that the student is an adult, he or she should really be the one to send that email to the professor or to have the conversation about course requirements.

You might be afraid that if you've been doing many things for your child over the years that a sudden withdrawal of this kind of help can lead to disaster. It's true. Unexpectedly pulling away supports isn't necessarily the best solution. You may be able to engage in a conscious process of easing out of the role that you have been playing in your child's life for so many years. Sit down and have a discussion about this, and make a plan together, so that you are both on the same page. Let your student take hold of the reins gradually, slowly building competence and independence. I know so many students who are highly intelligent, creative, and motivated learners who are struggling to become the independent adults that they long to be. If there is a way for you to help your child to become more independent, it is by encouraging them to step into the cockpit themselves, so that they can really start to soar.

Where it Hurts

As part of this process of letting a student take the reins, there will most likely be times when your college student may do something that will not only leave you feeling confused and frustrated but may also lead to consequences that will hit you where it hurts the most – right in the heart and right in the wallet. When it's a challenge to manage time, prioritize activities, and get motivated to complete tasks, missing important deadlines is a frequent and unfortunate result. It's hard enough to deal with the everyday consequences of these challenges, such as a lower GPA due to missed assignments. It's even harder to know what to do or how to feel when your college student misses something important and then you are stuck paying for it.

Making it through a college environment that is designed for typical students can be like sliding through an obstacle course covered in grease. If you are able to acknowledge ahead of time that navigating college may not be as straight-forward for your student as it is for most others, you may find the patience and compassion that you will need to get through these challenges.

The heart of this particular problem lies in the fact that *college ain't cheap.* You know it, and I know it. Most students and their families pay dearly for their education, even at public institutions. And when you're paying so much for an education, time is money. So, let's say that your student misses an important assignment in an important class, and therefore receives a failing grade. This class is a prerequisite for several other courses in their major. If they want to continue on, they will need to pay the costs of taking the course again. Or, perhaps the adjustment to freshman year gets the best of them, and due to their grades, they lose their scholarship money. Now, the family is bearing the financial strain of paying more for college than they may have planned.

So, the question here is how can you avoid losing it when these things happen? And how can you keep your relationship with your child from suffering from the effects of blame and shame? I would recommend that, at the very least, doing some mental and emotional (if not financial) preparation for these kinds of outcomes may soften the blow a bit. Making it through a college environment that is designed for typical students can be like sliding through an obstacle course covered in grease. You may feel that the system is designed to deal out setback after setback to students with ADHD. Of course, that doesn't make it any less frustrating if college is taking longer than planned or the fees are adding up. If you are able to acknowledge ahead of time that navigating college may not be as straight-forward for your student as it is for most others, you may find the patience and compassion that you will need to get through these challenges.

That River in Egypt

While some parents are busy doing anything and everything to support their college student, still other parents fall into another pattern at the opposite extreme. One of the other common issues facing students with ADHD is the sense that some people just don't believe that the challenges they face are real. Of course, I'm talking about denial. For some parents, it may be hard to admit that your son or daughter has ADHD. A new diagnosis may cause parents to need to readjust the image that they have of their own child. This is particularly true for students who may not have struggled as much in high school, but then, upon starting their first semester in college, they suddenly find themselves overwhelmed by the demands of the university environment and the lack of structure in their schedules. There are many people who go through life quite easily and successfully until they reach some stage that is especially challenging. Once they reach the limits of their coping mechanisms, they suddenly feel as though they have hit a wall. The transition from high school to college can certainly be like this for many students. So, it is not surprising that some parents will struggle to understand an ADHD diagnosis for their child who may have seemed to be doing just fine all the way through high school. They may seek to deny this as a reality, and instead blame the student for their difficulties.

From the student's perspective, it is extremely difficult to be constantly overwhelmed by the many challenges that they face in school. But it might be even harder to endure the challenges of going through school as a different type of learner and then, on top of that, to be told that they are really just overwhelmed because they are not putting in enough effort. In reality, many students with ADHD are putting in much more effort than their peers and are still struggling to keep their heads above water. Parents who deny the reality of ADHD are implying, or sometimes saying outright, that the student is lazy, unmotivated, or stupid. To hear that from educators over the course of our schooling is bad enough, but to hear these negative messages from our parents can be heartbreaking.

If you are having a tough time accepting the reality of an ADHD diagnosis, my message to you is simple: **the struggle is real!** ADHD is real. I know, you may have read many conflicting opinions about this. Even despite all the research that has been done surrounding ADHD in the past few decades, there are still "experts" out there, spouting misinformation in newspaper columns and seminars. They may tell you that it is all just a problem due to bad parenting or lazy students. But I assure you, denying the reality of ADHD-related challenges is not going to help your student get through college, and it most definitely won't help your relationship with your child! One thing that will help, however, is listening to your college student, coming to a place of understanding, and then supporting them as they try to get through it.

Excuses, Excuses!

Once you have accepted that ADHD truly does make it difficult for your college student to remember things, to get motivated for his or her classes, and to get work done without procrastinating, it can be easy to fall into the trap of using it as an excuse for anything and everything. You've stopped blaming them for their mistakes, but you may have gone from constantly nagging at your son or daughter to get their homework done to just accepting that the homework wasn't done because he or she has ADHD. There must be a way of understanding that the challenges are real without relaxing the standards for their performance. Our kids are quite savvy, and they learn very quickly how to play to our weaknesses. If they know that we won't hold them accountable for something, then they may take every opportunity to play us, using ADHD as an excuse for why this or that project was handed in late or why they were not handing in homework assignments.

As someone who has ADHD, I truly do understand how difficult it can be sometimes to get that homework done. However, as a professor, I absolutely expect all my students to get theirs done on time. Just because we have ADHD doesn't mean we can give up or not do what is required of us. This just doesn't fly in the work world! If we don't get our work done, we let down our team members, and we could lose our jobs. We can, instead, without blaming them, find teachable moments and work on finding solutions.

When I run my meetings with groups of students with ADHD, inevitably, some of the participants will stroll in 10 or 15 minutes late. On one occasion, two students admitted that they were late because they *both* lost their dorm keys and had to spend several minutes looking for them before they could leave. We used this as an opportunity to talk about how ADHD can affect us when we are in college and at work: when we show these behaviors, others will perceive us negatively, and assume that we are unmotivated or uncaring, even when this may be the farthest thing from the truth. Yes, we can be very forgetful, misplace things, and show up late. But once we know this about ourselves, we can put strategies in place to help us avoid these problems. We brainstorm strategies: some of us set our watches ten to fifteen minutes fast, or we tell ourselves that the meeting starts 15 minutes earlier than it really does. Others create a specific place where they put their keys every single time they walk in the door, or even place a tracker device on their keys so that they can find them using their smart phones. We seek ways to hold ourselves to the same high standard that is expected of everyone.

We may have to work three times as hard to get the simple things done sometimes, but we need to do anything and everything in our power to find a way to get these things done, without all the excuses. As a parent, I would encourage you to help your student develop a responsibility mindset. Understand, but don't excuse. And in your discussions, help your child to put in place strategies and coping mechanisms that can help to both understand and take ownership of behaviors in the most productive way.

The Balancing Act

As you may have noticed, many of my observations have concerned parents who have reacted to the student's diagnosis of ADHD by going to one extreme or another. While one seeks to ignore and erase the reality of the ADHD diagnosis, another accepts the reality of the diagnosis, but then enables the student to use ADHD as an excuse. Still another understands very well the challenges that come with ADHD and tries to help the student compensate by doing everything for them. These behaviors are most often based in a desire for the child to succeed, but all of these patterns can create problems for college students. It is not my intention to fault you for feeling this way. As parents, we all want the best for our children, and we want them to succeed. Of course, we do. My hope, though, is that as parents, you may find a place more in the center, so that we do not unintentionally hold back the student from developing into the independent adult that he or she is becoming.

Finding a way to support our college students in a healthy way can feel like we are sending our children out onto a high wire on a unicycle. We may be afraid that they will lose their balance and tumble the long distance to the ground. We may want to hold on tight, or to put up a safety net in case they fall. But the reality is, this is not our circus anymore, and college students must find a way to perform without all the supports that they once had. But most tightrope walkers use a long pole as they walk across the wire. They are using a tool that helps them create their own sense of balance. In a sense, this is what we, as parents and educators should seek to give our students with ADHD. We can't go out there on the rope with them. They just need to learn to use the tools that will help them to walk on their own.

Cheerleaders

So, now that we are encouraging our students to get out there and face the world on their own, where does that leave parents? As odd as it may sound, being on the sidelines may be just the perfect place for you to cheer on your students as they learn to navigate college as young adults. The emotions of students with ADHD can be somewhat like an Achilles heel; even a very small emotional injury can take them down into the depths of discouragement. When mistakes leave your student feeling demoralized, distressed, or depressed, it is so important for them to know that their parents are still rooting for them.

Seeing college-aged students with ADHD through a strength-based lens may help you to encourage them to follow their passions in unconventional ways, help them to take that unexpected leap for innovation, or break the mold with their out-of-the-box thinking. By embracing their strengths, you help them reach their true creative potential.

In my experience, the very best motivation for students with ADHD is encouragement from people who truly do believe in their potential. The negative messages that our students receive throughout their school experiences often pool together to form an immense swamp of self-doubt that can be hard to wade through. I can't emphasize enough the importance of someone cheering them on as they strive to make it to the other side. This may be the one case where going overboard really can be helpful. Parents can be the ones who provide the encouragement needed to cancel out the negativity that so often seems to be pouring in from all sides.

Untapped Power

Beyond the ins and outs of helping a student manage the daily challenges of college independently, I want to share one final message with you that may give you hope and even inspire you to see your college student in a brand-new light. If you have read this book from front to back, you already know that I believe that students with ADHD are an as-yet untapped source of powerful creativity. The unique way that our brains function gives us the ability to gather information and make new connections between things that would seem unrelated to most people; when we take on the role of explorer, inventor, and innovator, we have the potential to bring real value to our companies, to our families, to our society, and even to our world.

You may have been told repeatedly that your child would not succeed in school, or even in life. You may have been pressured into lowering your expectations for your child's potential due to a diagnosis that was presented as both a deficiency and a disorder. Now you know that despite what you have been told, this narrative is incomplete. The tremendously powerful creativity of people with ADHD traits can be nurtured and leveraged for success.

As you already know, people with ADHD traits can be forces of nature; our endless creative energy is almost unstoppable once it is unleashed. Now that you are aware of the innate strengths that are wired into these students' very being, you may find new ways to support their growth while leveraging their strengths. Seeing college-aged students through this lens may help you to encourage them to follow their passions in unconventional ways, help them to take that unexpected leap for innovation, or break the mold with their out-of-the-box thinking. By embracing their strengths, you help them reach their true creative potential.

- 7 -

A CHALLENGE TO EDUCATORS

If you are an educator, this chapter is for you. You may have been asked to read it by a friend, family member, or a student who feels newly inspired about his or her creative potential and wants to share this new-found optimism with you. You may be skeptical about the reality of ADHD and reluctant to implement accommodations in your classroom, even though they are required by law, because you think that it gives certain students an unfair advantage over others. Or, you may be seeking information because you care deeply about your students, you want to make your teaching more accessible to them, and you want to be the best educator you can be. For whatever reason you have picked up this book, I would like to both thank you for your willingness to consider a new point of view and also challenge you to think critically about your own and your institution's environment, ingrained attitudes, and educational practices.

My goal for this chapter is not to give you specific tips about the implementation of particular accommodations or teaching methods in your courses. Rather, I aim to share my experiences and stimulate a dialogue about how we can better serve a vulnerable and underrepresented group of students in our colleges and universities. Many times, educators accustomed to the constant deluge of new initiatives are resistant to change, and we cling to our traditional teaching methods. How can we move beyond our defensive preservation of the status quo and challenge the common practices that may not only be ineffective teaching methods, but in fact may also discriminate against the diverse thinkers that populate our classes?

By embracing instructional methods that encourage exploration, allow diversity of thought, and emphasize creative problem-solving, you may be helping to create a college experience that is not only more accessible to many types of learners, but also nurtures tomorrow's change-makers, entrepreneurs, and innovators.

As we move forward, we must be willing to break the inertia of habit and reconsider our preconceptions about the student populations that have faced barrier after barrier in seeking higher education. I hope that this book has inspired you to gain a better understanding of your students with ADHD so that you can help them reach their highest potential.

For many students who have struggled through the education system, there are always stories of that "one teacher" who made a difference in their life by believing in them, challenging them to achieve, and honoring their strengths. As educators, we have a huge amount of power to influence the lives of struggling students in myriad ways; factors as simple as the environment that we create can make or break the educational experience for a student with ADHD. Furthermore, by embracing instructional methods that encourage exploration, allow diversity of thought, and emphasize creative problem-solving you may be helping to create a college experience that is not only more accessible to many types of learners, but also nurtures tomorrow's change-makers, entrepreneurs, and innovators.

Invisibility

Our institutions have come far in recognizing the ways in which common practices can be discriminatory against various groups of people. Simply making buildings accessible through the addition of access ramps and elevators quite literally opens the doors of higher education to those who may have been historically shut out of the classroom. The provision of Braille textbooks, the availability of audio resources, technological advances in voice-to-text software, and the presence of service dogs on campus are other examples of how making changes at the institutional level can make education more accessible to all types of learners. Still, cognitively diverse learners, such as students with ADHD may feel that the "invisible" nature of their difference leaves them out in the cold.

Some professors, who may not be able to "see" why students with ADHD are struggling, may be resistant to providing accommodations in the classroom, and may feel that they are being asked to do more work, or that they are being asked to provide an unfair advantage to some. Many students find themselves continually bumping up against the conscious or unconscious attitudes of professors who harbor the stubborn belief that students with ADHD are simply stupid, lazy, and unmotivated. If the professor can't *see* the cause of the difficulty, then it must be made up, a simple crutch for a student who refuses to do the work. Educators must increase their comprehension of ADHD in order to realize that the student's brain is wired in a way that is often in direct conflict with the expectations and requirements of the classroom. Simply taking the time to consider up-to-date information about ADHD allows the educator to move beyond blame and into awareness and compassion.

Despite the scientific advances and a dramatic increase in knowledge about ADHD in recent years, the abundance of conflicting information, the persistence of misinformation about ADHD, and the prevailing negative narrative about ADHD contribute to the stigmatization and misunderstanding of students with ADHD in the classroom and in life. Over the course of their school years, students report feeling misunderstood and stigmatized by their educators. Many college students are, therefore, unwilling to disclose their ADHD status or seek the educational accommodations that are legally available to them. This sense that students must hide their diagnosis of ADHD further compounds students' feeling of invisibility on college campuses.

The Student Experience

As someone who has gone through the education system with ADHD, I know all too well the feeling of struggling through courses that were presented in ways that were inaccessible to me. Grappling with memorization of long lists of facts and difficulties with working memory, coupled with attentional bias (the ability to sustain intense concentration only on topics of interest), and diffuse attention (the tendency to pay attention to many things at once, which may impede focus in a classroom setting) can all deeply alter the experience of learning and studying. We learners with ADHD may wrestle with focusing during long lectures, have difficulty taking organized notes during class, and have trouble getting our homework completed and turned in. We may spend a great deal of additional time studying for our exams, and yet still not perform as well as we should. The result of all these challenges is the agonizingly frustrating experience of receiving grades that do not reflect our intelligence and potential.

These battles only continue when we are met by professors who may not fully understand the reality of our cognitive differences and how they may affect our learning process. We may come to our professors seeking help, but then run into a wall. Instead of compassion, we many times find educators who perceive us as slackers. Our professors may think that we are looking for an unfair advantage over our classmates or think that if we make mistakes or miss assignments that we just don't care. Ultimately, we may feel so embarrassed and ashamed that we may not bother to correct them.

These issues are often reflected in our GPAs, which further negatively impact our chances for success through the loss of scholarships, internships, and other opportunities that are typically reserved for those with the highest GPAs. Being told over and over that we are "deficient" or "disordered" is devastating, and the loss of self-esteem that comes from negative experiences in our schools often deepens the cut. If we make it to college at all, we are often wounded and scarred by our experiences. Still, college students with ADHD often possess a characteristic resilience that allows them to continue striving toward their goals despite this barrage of negative feedback.

An Alternate Ending

If you have read the earlier portions of this book, you have already discovered that there is indeed a more hopeful narrative that provides an alternate ending to the story that we have all been told. The genetic inheritance of what is currently known as ADHD, allows us to gather large amounts of information, explore new territory, take the risks necessary to do the unexpected, consider multiple solutions to complex problems, and to pursue our goals with boundless energy once we have set our sights on a goal. It is true that we tend to not follow the conventional path. Students in science courses are often asked to follow a set of procedures, but those of us who tend to think in more divergent patterns may pursue multiple pathways to a solution, or even multiple solutions to a problem. If we are evaluated on our ability to follow the linear steps outlined for us by the professor, we may fail.

But failure is not the only option. If we are evaluated on our ability to think creatively and arrive at novel solutions, we may not only thrive academically, but in fact be encouraged to take these novel solutions to the next level through patenting our creations, marketing our solutions, and exploring entrepreneurship. If you only hear the one story about the student who couldn't achieve, then you won't ever find a way to see what that same student actually can do. And while every student won't amaze you, be assured that some of your students with ADHD can and will knock your socks off if you get to know their unique strengths and give them ways to put them into action.

I know that I have presented you with what may be considered a controversial point of view. You may be feeling a bit skeptical about this or overwhelmed by what seems like *just one more burden* to be added to the already overwhelming responsibilities of an educator. Perhaps some of you are leaning back in your chair, thinking that this sounds wonderful, but you'll believe it when you see it. Sometimes it is difficult to fully understand and embrace new concepts without a hands-on experience that provides real-life context for learning.

Over the past few years, we have addressed this need to provide educators with the experiences necessary to foster understanding of the unique abilities of our neurodiverse students by inviting teachers to participate in our National Science Foundation-funded summer program for undergraduate students with ADHD. In the summer of 2016, two public school educators joined our activities as Research Experiences for Teachers (RET) Fellows, and their observations were presented at the 2017 American Society for Engineering Education (ASEE) conference. Their experiences, much like those of our student participants, were transformative.

The 2016 RET Fellows included one elementary school teacher and one secondary school teacher. For six weeks, these educators participated in engineering research activities, attended workshops, and engaged in roundtable discussions along with the student participants in the Research Experiences for Undergraduates (REU) Program. This in-depth experience provided the opportunity for teachers to spend a great deal of time with students with

ADHD outside of the confines of a traditional classroom and observe their performance in a specialized, strength-based learning environment.

They observed that students with ADHD can, in fact, thrive, given the right environment. In this case, the students found their niche in engineering research, which provides a unique opportunity for students to pursue solutions to complex problems. The teachers observed that the students thrived in great part because their innate strengths were valued and nurtured throughout the program. This specialized environment allowed students with ADHD to contribute in meaningful ways to high-level scientific research while also significantly increasing the self-confidence of the participants.

As the program came to a close, our RET Fellows reflected on these observations in relation to both their teaching and the education system. The teachers envisioned an educational system where student strengths are valued, and where creativity is nurtured through hands-on learning, exploration, and problem solving. They acknowledged the need for educators to examine their perceptions of neurodiverse individuals and to redesign both the learning process and the academic environment to better serve the diverse thinking styles of all students.

What We Can Do

Now that you understand that we, as educators, are in a unique position to intervene in the educational experiences of our students with ADHD, we are faced with some important questions. What can we do to improve the education system for our students? Or, even more precisely, what are we willing to do? How far are we willing to go to make changes that will make life better for our students?

First, it is important to note that students with ADHD are legally entitled to protections under Section 504 of the Rehabilitation Act of 1973, IDEA (Individuals with Disabilities Education Act), and ADA (Americans with Disabilities Act). The follow-through on this is fairly straight-forward. Students may need extended time on exams, outlines of the class notes, or modified assignments. These types of accommodations are legally required, and therefore, it is up to educators to learn about reasonable accommodations that are to be provided according to the law. But the reality of our situation is often a bit more complex than this.

To receive accommodations in courses, students must provide evidence of a disability to an office on campus. Still, we know that many students with ADHD have declined to register with their Center for Students with Disabilities due to the associated stigma and negative attitudes from their professors. Some of these students are exceptional in more than one way; they may struggle with attentional difficulties in class, but still have a very high IQ. Some students with ADHD traits may be extraordinarily gifted in some areas. Many of these students would rather double down on their work and struggle through on their own than be accused of faking a disability to get ahead. This leaves one segment of our students particularly vulnerable, since they are essentially invisible to the institution in terms of their need for accommodations in classes. The question, then, is how can we make our courses more accessible for all learners, even if they have declined to label themselves as a student with a disability?

While standard accommodations are an important part of this discussion, it is also key to consider how we as educators can better design our courses using some of the principles of UDL (Universal Design for Learning). There are many sources available online and in print that may allow you to learn more about this. The principles include using multiple modes of presentation, the use of instructional technologies, and varied learner supports. In short, if you always lecture using text-only PowerPoint presentations, you may need to shake things up a bit!

Challenging our own preconceived notions about our students will allow us to create a more welcoming and nurturing environment for them. If we approach our students with openness and compassion, while encouraging diverse thinking and learning styles, we may have the ability to drastically alter the education system for all students, regardless of who they are.

Additionally, we can support our students by providing opportunities for them to access their internal motivation system. Students with ADHD have a nervous system that only activates attention under certain conditions, primarily when the person is personally interested in the topic. This means that incorporating some element of personal choice into coursework may allow these students to activate their engagement in the course. Is there an element of independent study or exploration that can be incorporated in the course? Are there multiple ways that students can be evaluated to demonstrate their understanding? For example, instead of writing a twenty-page paper, students may choose to paint something that illustrates their understanding of the material and then present it to the class with an audio recording of them explaining what the painting represents. Other examples include allowing a student to create a website for their education class, or to code a video game that explores basic economics principles.

The possibilities here are truly endless, but only if we allow ourselves to go beyond the assumed traditional, overly structured educational practices that are built into our institutions. These changes may take some effort on our part, but they may make an enormous difference in the lives of our students. Beyond this, simply changing our minds and challenging our own preconceived notions about our students will allow us to create a more welcoming and nurturing environment for them. If we approach our students with openness and compassion, while encouraging diverse thinking and learning styles, we may have the ability to drastically alter the education system for all students, regardless of who they are.

Pushback

One of the goals of my research is to broaden the impact of my findings through various outreach and educational efforts. Because my focus is on improving the educational experience and successful outcomes for students with ADHD, bringing my message to other educators is a pivotal part of the process. How can the education system improve if educators continue to be underinformed about the issues affecting so many of their students? Despite the immense importance of educators furthering their understanding about the needs of diverse learners and engage in critical reflection about the education system, the reality is that some teachers and professors *just don't want to go there.*

Since the majority of the feedback from students and their families has been tremendously positive, I was shocked to discover that the most pushback and the most negative feedback that I received was from other educators. I have been told that students with ADHD are "fundamentally incapable of success" and that my research is simply a "distraction" from other, more worthwhile engineering research. However, we know in our hearts that this is untrue. We are here to learn, and we are often deeply passionate about our studies, but we still struggle to function effectively in such a rigidly structured environment because we are working in a system that was built for neurotypical minds. Since we are wired differently than most, we seek change in the education system so that we can succeed and reach our potential.

It seems that some educators have closed their minds to hearing this message because it both challenges their understanding of ADHD and implicates the education system in a failure to meet the needs of all students. In short, many educators react defensively and seem unwilling to try to bring about change. I know that I am probably upsetting some of you, but I am willing to take that risk because the well-being of our students is at stake. So, even if what I am saying makes you feel uncomfortable or angry, please consider keeping an open mind. We both know, since you have nearly finished reading this book, that you are one of the few who may be open to hearing this message and willing to recognize and face the challenges that come along with it. Our students need you to fight for them and advocate for change within the educational system.

Research shows that many individuals with ADHD traits are highly intelligent and highly creative. Our divergent thinking and unparalleled risk-taking abilities give us a unique potential to innovate, to push for change, and do the unexpected. However, traditional education methods, especially in STEM courses, rely heavily on linear thinking, rote memorization, and single-mode presentation and communication styles.

The conflict between common instructional practices and the functions of the ADHD brain creates a barrier for non-standard thinkers that can bar them from educational success. In short, many of the ways that teaching and learning commonly take place and the practices that so many educators take for granted are biased against us. When the practices are widely supported at the institutional level, we are essentially set up to fail in higher educational due to wide-spread discriminatory practice in the classroom.

I know it is uncomfortable to hear someone say that educators may be implicated in discrimination against a vulnerable population of students, but please, hear me out. We have committed ourselves to work toward a better, more just world. We are careful to not use racially discriminatory words, examples, or content in our teachings. We take great care to ensure that our admissions practices are more equitable so that we can all benefit from the engaging dialogue stimulated by a diverse community that includes people of varied backgrounds and cultures, sexual orientations, and socioeconomic status, as well as those with physical and learning disabilities. It has become increasingly clear that the quality of our outcomes is better with the input of a group of diverse people. It is time to include cognitive diversity in our definition of valued contributors to our educational environment.

Challenging the Status Quo

We all want to believe that we have the best interests of our students at heart. Of course, most educators care deeply about their students and truly want them to succeed. Even still, the truth is that sometimes, without knowing it, many of our habits, along with our steadfast commitment to "the way things are done," may keep us from acknowledging the bias present in the daily practices of teaching and learning in a university setting.

The first step is just being willing to think critically about our daily educational practices. Which of our teaching techniques are essentially locking some students out of the learning process, and how can we better design our teaching? We can attend professional development sessions and workshops to learn more about cognitive diversity, accessible education, multiple modes of expression, Universal Design for Learning, and creative problem solving. We can talk to our students and really take the time to understand their experiences, to feel the pain of their struggles, and ask them what we can do to make things better. We can read more. We can join online groups on social media where we can hear what students and their families are experiencing. We need to put aside our current understanding and truly listen and learn from the experiences of others. It can be overwhelming to consider all the things that need to be done, but a small start is a beginning. As long as we are committed to making change, our students will feel the difference.

We may feel that our efforts are but tiny drops in the great sea of the education system, but when we make these small adjustments, others may feel inspired to do the same. Through the sharing of best practices with our colleagues, we may further spread these changes and make a difference for all our students. If we dare to challenge our personal status quo, we may succeed in contributing to large-scale systemic change that will benefit both individuals and society. By nurturing the strengths of our diverse group of learners and encouraging the creative risk-taking needed, we can make the leap toward finding novel solutions to the complex challenges that we are facing as a nation.

If we dare to challenge our personal status quo, we may succeed in contributing to large-scale systemic change that will benefit both individuals and society. By nurturing the strengths of our diverse group of learners and encouraging creative risk-taking, we can make the leap toward finding novel solutions to the complex challenges that we are facing as a nation.

ACKNOWLEDGEMENTS

Special thanks go to the National Science Foundation for their strong support of my research activities related to creativity and ADHD in engineering programs. My sincere appreciation goes to program managers Elliot Douglas, Donna Riley, and Mary Poats for their belief in both the merit and the impact of this research. With their support, we have built a program that has already made a tremendous difference in the lives of students with ADHD.

Also deserving thanks are Kazem Kazerounian, Ph.D., who supported my research; Sally Reis, Ph.D., whose understanding of gifted and twice-exceptional students has been key in the conception and formation of the ideas in this book; James C. Kaufman, Ph.D., and Joseph S. Renzulli, Ed. D., whose expertise in the field of creativity contributed greatly to this work; Susan Baum, Ph.D., who encouraged and inspired me to pursue this effort; and Joyce Kamanitz, M.D., who contributed to the formation of my research activities, supported and inspired me with her constant encouragement, and shared her expertise and insights about the content of this book.

Many thanks go to my wife, Sarira, who offered her endless support and keen insights; to my graduate students, who gave selflessly of their time and energy to provide valuable feedback about the content of this book; to Alexandra and Cathy Hain, for lending a critical eye to the review of this text; to the many parents who have reached out to me when they heard about my research, for helping me to understand both the intense need for and the potential impact of this message in the lives of students with ADHD; and to Connie Syharat, whose imaginative and creative writing made this book much more pleasant to read than the text that I might have drafted on my own.

To all, I give my most sincere thanks.

BIBLIOGRAPHY

Archer, Dale. "ADHD: The Entrepreneur's Superpower."
Forbes,
https://www.forbes.com/sites/dalearcher/2014/05/1
4/adhd-the-entrepreneurs-
superpower/#6ce7ca1c59e9.

———. *The ADHD Advantage: What You Thought Was a
Diagnosis May Be Your Greatest Strength.* New
York, NY, Penguin Random House LLC, 2015.

Boyd, Maggie. "Are General Education Courses a Waste of
Our Time?" Odyssey,
https://www.theodysseyonline.com/are-general-
education-courses-waste-of-our-time.

Branson, Richard. "Bill Gates and Why You Should Take
Notes." 2016.

———. "Keep Your Curiosity Alive." 2017.

———. "Richard Branson Reveals the Biggest Business
Risks He's Ever Taken." Independent,
https://www.additudemag.com/successful-people-
with-adhd-learning-disabilities/.

Brown, T.E. *Smart but Stuck: Emotions in Teens and Adults
with ADHD.* San Francisco, CA
Jossey-Bass, 2014.

Cox, David. "A Learning Disability Often Makes for a More
Visionary, Innovative Ceo." QUARTZ,
https://qz.com/413783/learning-disability-makes-
for-a-more-visionary-innovative-ceo/.

Craig, Russell J., and Joel H. Amernic. "Powerpoint
Technology and the Dynamics of Teaching."
Innovative Higher Education 31, no. 3 (2006): 147-
60.

Crawford, Aimee. "Bravo, Simone Biles for Taking a Stand
against ADHD Stigma." ESPN.com,
http://www.espn.com/espnw/voices/article/1760254
0/bravo-simone-biles-taking-stand-adhd-stigma.

"Decoding the Creative Genius of Leonardo Da Vinci." WBUR, http://www.wbur.org/onpoint/2017/10/17/decoding-the-creative-genius-of-leonardo-da-vinci.

Ding, Y.-C., H.-C. Chi, Deborah. Grady, Atsuyuki. Morishima, Judith R. Kidd, Kenneth K. Kidd, Pamela. Flodman, *et al.* "Evidence of Positive Selection Acting at the Human Dopamine Receptor D4 Gene Locus." *Proceedings of the National Academy of Sciences of the United States of America* 99, no. 1 (2002): 309-14.

Dodson, William. "3 Defining Features of Adhd That Everyone Overlooks." ADDitude, https://www.additudemag.com/symptoms-of-add-hyperarousal-rejection-sensitivity/.

Dutton, Judy. "On Your Mark, Get Set, Glow: 3 Inspiring Athletes with ADHD." ADDitude, https://www.additudemag.com/famous-athletes-with-adhd/.

Farrell, Rebecca. "How Virgin Produced Created Space for Creativity." https://www.virgin.com/entrepreneur/how-virgin-produced-created-space-creativity.

Grant, Adam. *Originals: How Non-Conformists Move the World.* New York, NY: Penguin Books, 2016.

Gritz, Jennie Rothenberg. "What's Wrong with the American University System." The Atlantic, https://www.theatlantic.com/entertainment/archive/2010/07/whats-wrong-with-the-american-university-system/60458/.

Haden, Jeff. "'Don't Look Down' Movie Review: The inside Story of Richard Branson's Hot Air Balloon Adventures." https://www.inc.com/jeff-haden/dont-look-down-movie-review-the-inside-story-of-richard-bransons-hot-air-balloon.html.

Hain, Catherine C., Turek, Wendy C., Zaghi, A. E., Hain, A. E. "Experiences of Pre-College Teachers Working with Undergraduate Engineering Students with

ADHD in Research Laborotories." In *2017 ASEE Annual Conference & Exposition*, New Orleans, LA, 2017.

Hallowell, Edward M., and John J. Ratey. *Driven to Distraction: Recognizing and Coping with Attention Deficit Disorder from Childhood through Adulthood.* New York, NY: Random House, Inc., 2011.

Hartmann, Thom. *ADHD and the Edison Gene: A Drug-Free Approach to Managing the Unique Qualities of Your Child.* Rochester, VT: Park Street Press, 2015.

———. *Adult ADHD: How to Succeed as a Hunter in a Farmer's World.* Rochester, VT: Park Street Press, 2016.

———. *Attention Deficit Disorder: A Different Perception.* 2 ed. Grass Valley, CA: Underwood Books, 1997.

Healey, Dione., and Julia J. Rucklidge. "An Investigation into the Relationship among ADHD Symptomatology, Creativity, and Neuropsychological Functioning in Children, Ch." *Child Neuropsychology* 12, no. 6 (2006): 421-38.

Hehir, Thomas, and Laura A. Schifter. *How Did You Get Here? Students with Disabilities and Their Journeys to Harvard.* Cambridge, MA: Harvard Education Press, 2015.

Isaacson, Walter. *Leonardo Da Vinci.* New York, NY: Simon & Schuster, 2017.

Isaacson, Walter. "The Lessons of Leonardo: How to Be a Creative Genius." The Wall Street Journal, https://www.wsj.com/articles/the-lessons-of-leonardo-how-to-be-a-creative-genius-1506690180.

Kidd, Celeste., and Benjamin Y. Hayden. "The Psychology and Neuroscience of Curiosity." *Neuron* 88, no. 3 (2015): 449-60.

"Learn from Richard Branson." https://www.creativelive.com/30-days-of-genius/richard-branson?via=html-freeform_1.

Leef, George. "The Terrible Erosion of the College Curriculum." Forbes,

https://www.forbes.com/sites/georgeleef/2013/11/07
/the-terrible-erosion-of-the-college-curriculum/.

Mainemelis, Charalampos., and Sarah. Ronson. "Ideas Are
Born in Fields of Play: Towards a Theory of Play and
Creativity in Organizational Settings." *Research in
Organizational Behavior* 27 (2006): 81-131.

Malone, Michael S. "Silicon Valley Survivor." The Wall
Street Journal,
https://www.wsj.com/articles/SB10001424052970203
517304574305901375020562.

Mlodinow, Leonard. 2018a. *Elastic: flexible thinking in a
time of change.* New York: Pantheon Books.

Mlodinow, Leonard. 2018b. "In Praise of A.D.H.D.". New
York Times, accessed 20 March 2018.
https://www.nytimes.com/2018/03/17/opinion/sund
ay/praise-adhd-attention-
hyperactivity.html?rref=collection%2
Fcolumn%2Fgray-
matter&action=click&contentCollection
=opinion&region=stream&module=stream_unit&ve
rsion=latest&contentPlacement=1&pgtype=collectio
n.

NVIDIA. "What Is Gpu-Accelerated Computing?"
http://www.nvidia.com/object/what-is-gpu-
computing.html.

Panksepp, Jaak. "Play, ADHD, and the Construction of the
Social Brain: Should the First Class Each Day Be
Recess?". *American Journal of Play* 1, no. 1 (2008):
55-79.

Pappas, Phill. *One Page at a Time: Getting through College
with ADHD.* Publisher: Author, 2010.

Paul, Annie Murphy. "The Protege Effect."
http://ideas.time.com/2011/11/30/the-protege-
effect/.

Puddu, Giannina, Paula Rothhammer, and Francisco
Rothhammer. "Genetic and Evolutionary
Contributions to the Etiology of Attention Deficit
Hyperactivity Disorder." *Current Genetic Medicine*

Reports 5, no. 1 (2017): 54-57. Published electronically March 2017. doi:https://doi.org/10.1007/s40142-017-0114-9, https://link.springer.com/article/10.1007/s40142-017-0114-9.

Rice, Louis. "Playful Learning." *Journal for Education in the Built Environment* 4, no. 2 (2009): 94-108.

Robinson, Ken. "Do Schools Kill Creativity?" https://www.ted.com/talks/ken_robinson_says_schools_kill_creativity?referrer=playlist-77.

Sarkis, Stephanie Moulton. *Making the Grade with Add: A Student's Guide to Succeeding in College with Attention Deficit Disorder,* Oakland, CA: New Harbinger Publications, Inc., 2008.

Shoot, Brittany. "The Stars Who Aligned ADHD with Success." ADDitude, https://www.additudemag.com/successful-people-with-adhd-learning-disabilities/.

"Simone Biles Says ADHD Is "Nothing to Be Ashamed Of"." In *In the News*: Understood.org, 2016.

Sinfield, Jacqueline. "ADHD and the 5 Second Rule." In *Untapped Brilliance,* 2016.

Swanson, J.M., Pamela. Flodman, James. Kennedy, M. Anne. Spence, Robert. Moyzis, Sabrina. Schuck, Michael. Murias, *et al.* "Dopamine Genes and ADHD". *Neuroscience and Biobehavioral Reviews* 24 (2000): 21-25.

"The Skills of Leonardo Da Vinci." http://www.lettersofnote.com/2012/03/skills-of-da-vinci.html.

Thompson, Melissa. "How These Companies Keep Creativity Flowing in the Workplace." Inc., https://www.inc.com/melissa-thompson/4-ways-these-companies-have-creative-workplaces.html.

Wang, E. Ding, Y.-C., P. Flodman, J.R. Kidd, K.K. Kidd, D.L. Grady, O.A. Ryder, M.A. Spence, J.M. Swanson, and R.K. Moyzis. "The Genetic Architecture of Selection at the Human Dopamine

Receptor D4 (DRD4) Gene Locus." *American Journal of Human Genetics* 74 (2004): 931-44.

Wasserstein, Jeanette., and Antoinette. Lynn. "Metacognitive Remediation in Adult ADHD. Treating Executive Function Deficits Via Executive Functions.". *Annals of the New York Academy of Sciences* 931 (2001): 376-84.

White, Holly A., and Priti Shah. "Creative Style and Achievement in Adults with Attention-Deficit/Hyperactivity Disorder." *Personality and Individual Differences* 50, no. 5 (2011): 673 - 77.

———. "Uninhibited Imaginations: Creativity in Adults with Attention-Deficit/Hyperactivity Disorder." *Personality and Individual Differences* 40, no. 6 (2006): 1121 - 31.

Williams, J., and E. Taylor. "The Evolution of Hyperactivity, Impulsivity and Cognitive Diversity." [In eng]. *J R Soc Interface* 3, no. 8 (Jun 2006): 399-413.

Wise, Roy A. "Dopamine, Learning and Motivation." *Nature Reviews. Neuroscience.* 5, no. 6 (2004): 483-94.

Wu, Jing., Haifan. Xiao, Hongjuan. Sun, Li. Zou, and L.-Q. Zhu. "Role of Dopamine Receptors in Adhd: A Systemic Meta-Analysis." *Molecular Neurobiology* 45 (2012): 605-20.

ABOUT THE AUTHOR

Arash Zaghi received his PhD in Civil Engineering with a focus on seismic design and novel methods in bridge construction. He is currently an Associate Professor in the Department of Civil and Environmental Engineering at the University of Connecticut. In addition to his dedication to engineering research, Dr. Zaghi has a passion for transforming engineering education by focusing on nurturing creativity. He has received national recognition for his studies on the creative potential of engineering students with ADHD. His work has been supported by multiple grants from the National Science Foundation, including the prestigious CAREER Award, which supports his efforts to foster innovation by increasing neurodiversity in engineering. His ultimate goal is to raise awareness of the potential of non-traditional thinkers to create novel solutions to the major challenges that we will face as a nation.

$19.95

ISBN 978-1-7325934-0-4

51995>

9 781732 593404

Made in United States
North Haven, CT
28 June 2024

54188678R10096